ST. PETERSBURG

ST. PETERSBURG

TEXT AND PHOTOGRAPHS BY STEVE RAYMER

Turner Publishing, Inc.

ATLANTA

Published by Turner Publishing, Inc.
A Subsidiary of Turner Broadcasting System, Inc.
1050 Techwood Drive, N.W.
Atlanta, Georgia 30318

First Edition 1 0 9 8 7 6 5 4 3 2 1

Library of Congress Cataloging-in-Publication Data

Raymer, Steve.
        St. Petersburg / text and photographs by Steve Raymer.
            p. cm.
        Includes bibliographical references and index.
        ISBN 1-878685-48-1
        1. Saint Petersburg (Russia)--Civilization. I. Title.
        II. Title: Saint Petersburg.
DK557.R39 1994
947'.453--dc20   94-8374
                                                                  CIP

Distributed by Andrews and McMeel
A Universal Press Syndicate Company
4900 Main Street
Kansas City, Missouri 64112

Walton Rawls, Vice President, Editorial
Katherine Buttler, Editor
Crawford Barnett, Editor
Charles O. Hyman, Picture Editor
Barbara Skinner, Field Producer and Researcher

Karen E. Smith, Book and Cover Design
Michael Walsh, Design Director
Nancy Robins, Production Director
Laszlo Kubinyi, Maps

Color separations and film preparation by Graphics International, Atlanta, Georgia.
Printing by Horowitz/Rae Book Manufacturers, Inc., Fairfield, New Jersey.

Printed in the U.S.A.

Archival Photo Credits:
Lenin Museum Archive, Moscow: p. 52
St. Petersburg Central State Archive of Cinema and Photo Documents:
        pp. 48, 49, 97, 100, 144, 157
Russian Information Agency: pp. 69, 74, 75

SCENE OF VICTORY *and political uprisings, Palace Square (previous pages) fronts the old Imperial Army General Staff Building and the Aleksandr Column—a monument to Russia's triumph over Napoleon in 1812. Washed in blue spotlights (right), the corps de ballet of the Mariinsky Opera and Ballet Theatre, formerly the Kirov, glide into the finale of* Giselle.

"Because, loving our city
And not winged freedom,
We preserved for ourselves
Its palaces, its fire and water."

ANNA AKHMATOVA
"PETROGRAD, 1919"
Anno Domini MCMXXI, 1922

CONTENTS

GOLD ADORNS
THE GATES
*of Catherine Palace, once
the favorite summer resi-
dence of the royal family,
in the St. Petersburg suburb
of Pushkin.*

A NAVY
TOWN
*from the start,
St. Petersburg has
always relied on
the sea for its
livelihood. On the
Neva River, the
crew of a Russian
navy submarine
musters on deck
for Navy Day
ceremonies.*

ALIVE WITH
GOLDEN MAPLES,
*Pavlovsk Palace and Park covers
3,750 acres (1,500 hectares) and
is one of the largest landscaped
parks in the world. Catherine the
Great built it for her son, the future
Tsar Paul I, and his German-born
wife, Maria Fyodorovna. With the
completion of a rail line between
St. Petersburg and Pavlovsk in
1838, the park became a popular
excursion for well-heeled
Russians—a tradition that endures
to this day for weekend picnicking
and cross-country skiing. From the
Winter Palace, (following page)
which is adorned with mythological
figures, a succession of tsars and
tsarinas ruled the Russian empire
for more than two hundred years
until Lenin, the Bolshevik revolutionary, moved the capital back to
Moscow in 1918. Between 2 and
5 A.M., more than a dozen draw-
bridges spanning the Neva open in
quick succession to allow convoys
of barges and tankers and the
occasional hulking submarine to
slip quietly on their way.*

FRESH
FROM A
BALTIC
STORM,
*snow brightens the
ninety-six neoclassi-
cal columns of the
Kazan Cathedral,
which was finished
in 1811 by
Aleksandr I, whose
ambitious construc-
tion schemes
transformed St.
Petersburg into a
European capital
whose architectural
lavishness rivaled
that of Rome.*

LIKE A
SCENE

*from nineteenth-
century Europe, the
Great Pond at
Catherine Palace
and Park in
Pushkin beckons
painters Natasha
and Aleksei
Malykh, both grad-
uates of the city's
academy of art.
The mosque-like
Turkish Bath
(background) was
the last of some
one hundred build-
ings and monu-
ments built on the
largest imperial-era
estate in Russia.*

COLORFUL
MOSAICS,
*seldom seen in
St. Petersburg,
grace the Church
of the Resurrection,
popularly called
the Saviour on the
Blood, built on the
exact place where
Tsar Aleksandr II
was assassinated
in 1881.*

"Here we at Nature's own behest
Shall break a window to the West,
Stand planted on the ocean level;
Here flags of foreign nations all
By waters new to them will call,
And unencumbered we shall revel."

ALEKSANDR PUSHKIN
THE BRONZE HORSEMAN: A TALE OF PETERSBURG, 1833

INTRODUCTION

Along the English Embankment, tucked between the soaring golden dome of St. Isaac's Cathedral and the brooding Neva River, sits St. Petersburg's most famous statue—a giant on horseback heroically posed with arm outstretched. The "bronze horseman" with the cold smile is Tsar Peter the Great, autocrat and visionary, who created St. Petersburg in a marshy wilderness between two rival empires.

St. Petersburg, the northernmost metropolis of its size, has lived and suffered for almost three hundred years under many rulers, yet Peter, more than any other, still dominates this old imperial capital, Russia's second largest city. His legacy is everywhere: in manicured gardens and lovingly restored palaces; in philharmonic halls exploding with applause; in some three hundred research centers made famous for discoveries in chemistry, genetics, and psychology and, more recently, for the high-tech secrets of space-based lasers, spy satellites, and exotic synthetic materials; and in the beehive of wharves, shipyards, and naval bases that link St. Petersburg to the world's great seas and once armed the Soviet navy for nuclear Armageddon with the West.

That this remarkable city of 5 million residents exists at all—a city of such splendor, creativity, and suffering—is testimony to Peter's iron will. To all who met him, the tsar had the coarse manners and hulking stride of a barbarian from the Slavic hinterlands. But in St. Petersburg, Peter was determined to imitate what he had seen in the great seaport cities of London and Amsterdam. And neither powerful Sweden nor a reluctant court in Moscow would stand in his way to awaken Russia, a backward Eurasian giant, from its medieval slumber. Peter's appetite for the fruits of Western civilization—the architecture, science, industry, customs, and dress of Europe—and especially his fascination for German culture and technological innovation—seemed as insatiable as his quest to vanquish Charles XII of nearby Sweden and secure a port for

COMMISSIONED BY EMPRESS CATHERINE *the Great in 1768, the gigantic* Bronze Horseman *likeness of Tsar Peter the Great took the French sculptor Etienne Falconet eleven years to complete.*

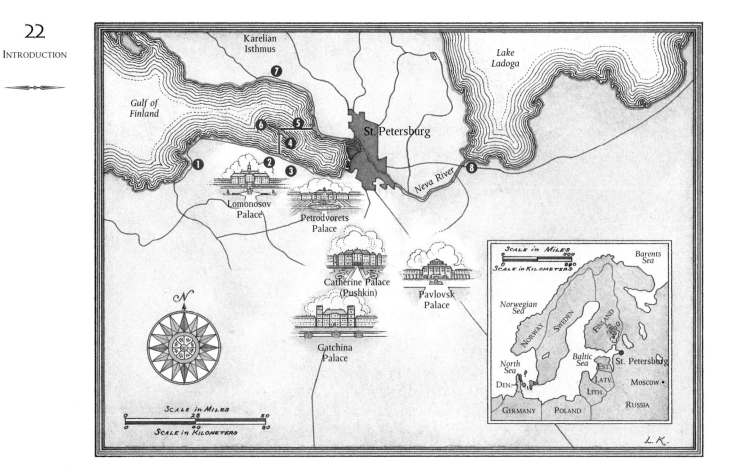

ST. PETERSBURG AND ITS ENVIRONS
❶ *Sosnovy Bor Atomic Power Station* ❷ *Lomonosov Palace*
❸ *Petrodvorets Palace* ❹ *Kronstadt* ❺ *Sea Barrier/Dam (under construction)*
❻ *Kotlin Island* ❼ *Zelenogorsk* ❽ *Schlüsselburg*

his new Baltic fleet. St. Petersburg was the progeny of both imperial ambitions.

Proclaiming himself leader for a new Russian age, Peter vowed to open in St. Petersburg that "window to the West" of Pushkin's lyric poem. In time, a city more European than Russian rose from the swamps of the Gulf of Finland—at an enormous cost in blood and treasure. Spread across the ice-covered islands of the Neva River delta, St. Petersburg did not grow from an ancient village where trade routes crossed and campfires burned through the millennia. It was, instead, born a capital less than a decade after its creation in 1703. Where the first Russian residents and emissaries from abroad saw only wilderness, Peter imagined a city at the doorstep of Europe, which was then entering the Age of Enlightenment. St. Petersburg's noble parentage gave it an aristocratic flair, a haughtiness

that remains part of the city's character today.

One of St. Petersburg's reigning aristocrats, Professor Dmitry Likhachev, has spent most of his long life studying the Russian character through ancient manuscripts. Now in his eighties, Likhachev is probably Russia's most respected living scholar. A moral giant often compared to the late Andrei Sakharov, Likhachev survived imprisonment in the Arctic under Stalin and the Nazi bombardment of Leningrad standing guard as a fire warden atop the roof of Pushkin House, a literary archive where the manuscripts of such great Russian writers as Pushkin, Dostoyevsky, and Lermontov are stored. Likhachev grew up with regular seats at the Mariinsky Theater, the old imperial ballet, and received a classical education in the German tradition at the K. I. Mai Gymnasium, St. Petersburg's finest secondary school before the Bolshe-

vik Revolution. Today he recalls his birthplace as a city where people read poetry in nearly every park or theater, and intellectuals gathered in university dormitories or elegant drawing rooms to discuss politics and literature in French, then the lingua franca of the capital. But the city Likhachev remembers has grown old and decrepit. Recent decades of neglect and decay have left it polluted and crime-ridden and the people dispirited. But Likhachev, who still loves his city, muses: "I was born in St. Petersburg, studied in Petrograd, worked in Leningrad, and hope to be buried in St. Petersburg."

This is more than a clever turn of phrase. Since the time Peter the Great gave this city the Germanic name "Sankt Piterburkh" in honor of his patron saint, it has assumed names that parallel the twists and turns of Russian history. When Russia declared war on Germany in 1914, Tsar Nicholas II, the last of Peter's line, Russified the city's name to Petrograd, or "City of Peter," cutting the linguistic link to the hated enemy. But changing the name of St. Petersburg could not mask the bankruptcy of Russia, then in the throes of a political and economic crisis. Nicholas II abdicated in 1917, and Russia withdrew from World War I to fight a civil war at home. The new Soviet government changed the city's name in 1924 to honor the father of Bolshevism, Vladimir Ilich Lenin, who incited revolution in St. Petersburg. The city remained Leningrad until September 6, 1991, when, with the Soviet state on the brink of collapse, the Russian Parliament quietly decreed a return to the name St. Petersburg. The news came shortly after 9 P.M., not as a televised news bulletin but in a fax unceremoniously delivered to the mayor's office at Mariinsky Palace not far from the towering equestrian statue of Peter the Great overlooking the Neva.

CAST FROM *Falconet's* Bronze Horseman, *a bust of Peter looms over the Russian Museum. Professor Dmitry Likhachev (left) reigns over St. Petersburg intellectuals, serving as the city's unofficial institutional memory. "I remember old Petersburg as a town of beautiful horses; of mirrors and shop windows that were beautiful, and the very intelligent faces on the street," recalls Likhachev. "You could tell a Petersburg woman by the way she walked—tall and straight."*

"Peter's powerful spirit and
Catherine's sovereign mind,
Achieved in one hundred years the labor
of slow centuries.**"**

PRINCE PETER VYAZEMSKY
AN NINETEENTH-CENTURY RUSSIAN POET

BORN A CAPITAL

Ten thousand years before Tsar Peter I claimed the Neva, it lay under more than 3,000 feet (1,000 meters) of ice. At about the same time that great civilizations flourished in the valleys of the Nile, Tigris, and Euphrates, a receding glacier left a vast sea—the Baltic—and flooded the territory of modern-day St. Petersburg. The Neva, a mere youngster in geological time, acquired its shape when Alexander the Great ruled much of Europe and Asia. Nomadic Finns fished the river and surrounding swamps, but they never settled in the endless, sometimes poisonous marshes beyond the banks of the Neva. All they left behind were remnants of their language, including the Finnish word for mud—Neva.

In its first incarnation, St. Petersburg was born a small river fort only seven degrees south of the Arctic Circle in a climate so harsh that many Russians still consider it unfit for everyday living. Nearly everyone in St. Petersburg complains about the weather, especially about the cyclones that blow in on short notice from the Gulf of Finland, an arm of the Baltic. Somber winter days make Petersburgers feel that they are living in a damp Arctic dungeon. Like bears in hibernation, they sleep more.

As autumn brings the chill of October and November, fierce Baltic Sea cyclones race across the shallow Gulf of Finland toward St. Petersburg, turning a thin slate-blue sky gray in minutes and churning up waves 18 feet (5.5 meters) high. Scientists report that these storms can race the 250 miles (402 kilometers) from Tallinn, the Estonian capital near the mouth of the gulf, to St. Petersburg in as little as five hours. The tidal waves, called "long waves" by Petersburgers, roll up the Neva estuary into St. Petersburg. The city, delicately balanced atop forty-two islands surrounded

ICE FISSURES
trail toward the Peter and Paul Fortress and the slender golden spire of the Saints Peter and Paul Cathedral, where more than thirty tsars and princes, including Peter the Great, are buried. The fortress was designed by Peter to protect the city from the Swedes, but soon lost its military significance and served as a political prison for about two hundred years.

CHAPTER ONE

and intersected by eighty-six rivers, streams, and canals, is no match for the Baltic's fury. Such storms as these moved the novelist Fyodor Dostoyevsky to write a century ago in *The Double*:

> *It was an awful November night—wet, foggy, rainy, snowy, teeming with colds in the head, fevers, swollen faces, quinseys, inflammations of all kind and description—teeming, in fact, with all the gifts of a Petersburg in November. The wind howled in the deserted streets, lifting up the black water of the [Fontanka] canal above the rings on the bank . . . . Snow and rain were falling both at once. Lashed by the wind, streams of rainwater spurted almost horizontally, as though from a fireman's hose, pricking and stinging the faces of the luckless.*

ON VASILY-EVSKY ISLAND, *institutes, libraries, and museums along University Embankment embody Peter's dream of modernizing Russia. One of Peter's greatest legacies is the modern Russian navy. A patrol boat (lower left) slips through the fog on Neva River.*

Over the years, the uncontrolled Neva has been merciless in its rage. When the water rises more than 13 feet (4 meters), St. Petersburg's historic core is under water—something that has happened nearly three hundred times since 1703. In 1721, Peter himself nearly drowned in floodwaters on Nevsky Prospekt. A flood on November 7, 1824—considered the city's worst and immortalized by Aleksandr Pushkin in his poem *The Bronze Horseman*—killed 569 people and destroyed 300 buildings.

But St. Petersburg suited Peter's needs, the costs be damned. And damned, indeed, were tens of thousands of Russian slaves and Swedish prisoners of war who died imposing Peter's will on the hostile Baltic marshes. Damned, too, were scores of diplomats, noblemen, and their families, who were commanded by the tsar to move to the flood-prone frontier outpost, which was cut off from the Russian mainland much of the year. The persistent tsar relocated his reluctant court from Moscow in 1712 and made St. Petersburg capital of a new Russian empire that already stretched to the Pacific Ocean.

Even today the city born of Peter's reckless vision does not easily beckon sailors or travelers. Beyond the Baltic fog and low clouds that hang over St. Petersburg on all but the fairest of days, there appears a low-rise city of slender golden spires, pastel-colored palaces, sweeping public buildings, and faceless sub-

urbs that eventually meet the great northern forests. No skyscrapers crowd this horizon.

Facelifts already have renewed many of St. Petersburg's great palaces, churches, and imperial government buildings that Peter and his successors built—and that others, notably Hitler's legions, destroyed so wantonly. St. Petersburg today stands frozen in time, a monument to the tsars, their European architects, and the Russian workers who together created a city amid the scattered islands and deep channels of the Neva River delta, where once there were only swamps.

The great Russian cities of Novgorod, Pskov, and Moscow had earlier built forts in this northern wilderness for territorial defense. But Sweden fiercely contested Russian control of the Neva delta, gaining dominance over the Baltic in 1617 after three hundred years of war. Less than a century later, Peter launched a campaign to wrest control of the strategic Neva from the Swedes. Only then could he build a mighty Baltic fleet and an ice-free port for trade with the West.

In the winter of 1702–3, Russian forces took the Swedish fort of Noteburg on Lake Ladoga at the headwaters of the Neva. Peter renamed it Schlüsselburg—"Key Town," or more to the point, key to the Baltic. Leading his navy of sixty boats loaded with troops and siege guns down the river, Peter attacked the Swedish garrison Nyenskans. The Swedes retreated on May 12, 1703, and a triumphant Peter ordered the keys of the two Swedish forts nailed to their gates, symbols that survive today on St. Petersburg's coat of arms.

On May 16 that same year, Peter laid the founda-

tion for the Peter and Paul Fortress on Hare Island near where the Neva divides into two main branches. Peter, legend says, dug two clumps of dirt with a bayonet, and laying the sod crosswise, proclaimed: "Here shall be a town." But, with the Swedish navy still prowling the Baltic coast, Peter changed the site of his future capital three times.

In 1704, Peter ordered residents to move closer to his fleet at Kronstadt, the rough naval fortress on Kotlin Island. But lacking a seafaring tradition, Russians disregarded the tsar and clustered instead on Petrograd Island a few yards (meters) north of the Peter and Paul Fortress.

It was not until Peter thrashed the army of Charles XII at Poltava in 1709 that his new city spread downstream to more promising islands in the Neva. (Eventually St. Petersburg would leap the Neva to the mainland of Russia itself.) "Now, indeed," wrote Peter on the evening after the battle of Poltava in the eastern Ukraine, "we can lay the foundation of Sankt Piterburkh." Flushed with victory, Peter returned with a vision for a maritime city on 4,000-acre (1,600-hectare) Vasilyevsky Island—largest in the Neva delta. His bold plan called for a European-style city of grand canals modeled after the Dutch seaport of Amsterdam. But the tsar's ambition to reproduce Amsterdam on the Gulf of Finland would fail miserably.

Peter looked to Europe for an architect, settling on a thirty-seven-year-old Frenchman named Jean-Baptiste Alexandre LeBlond. The most ambitious part of LeBlond's project called for a grid of parallel streets

ONE OF THE ALLEGORICAL FIGURES

(above) that represent the great Russian rivers rests beneath a brick-red Rostral Column on the Strelka, the eastern point of Vasilyevsky Island and once the city's commercial center. Often called the museum quarter, the Strelka's former Customs House and nearby warehouses are the site of the Institute of Russian Literature and museums of literature, zoology, and soil science. Across the Neva, in Palace Square (facing page), the faint half-light of winter outlines mighty St. Isaac's Cathedral.

BIRTHPLACE OF *modern Russian science, the Kunstkammer (facing page) became Russia's first museum. Chemist and astronomer Mikhail Lomonosov started Russia's first observatory in its fifth-floor cupola, while the main building housed Peter the Great's collection of "freaks and curiosities" gathered on his trips abroad. On Nevsky Prospekt (below), shoppers pay little notice to St. Petersburg's architectural glories, contending instead with gale-force winds and rising street crime.*

and intersecting canals that would cut through the marshes and bogs. The dirt from canal construction would be used as landfill, an idea that subsequent generations of architects successfully adopted, raising St. Petersburg more than 8 feet (2.5 meters) since Peter's day. LeBlond's plan called for two grand canals running the length of Vasilyevsky Island and twelve smaller ones—all large enough to accommodate two passing boats. But Peter was to be bitterly disappointed with the canals of Vasilyevsky Island. His involvement in distant wars and travels to European capitals kept the tsar absent often and thus allowed his best friend and the city's governor general, Prince Aleksandr Menshikov, to sabotage LeBlond's plan. Having been given most of Vasilyevsky as a present by Peter, Menshikov erected a massive, three-story mansion of his own and fought the prospect of sharing the forested estate. He had his own ideas for the island.

On Peter's return to the capital in 1718, he was "struck dumb with astonishment," wrote eighteenth-century historian J. V. Stahlin-Storckburg. Two boats could not pass on the canals and some canals were already silting up with mud. Peter personally measured the canals against the original plans for Amsterdam. Not a single one matched. An enraged Peter exclaimed: "The devil take the undertaking—all is spoiled," and stalked off. Drained by the cost of the two-decade-long Great Northern War with Sweden, Peter cut his losses and abandoned the canals. Today, only parts of the original canals remain on Vasilyevsky Island, and streets laid out as numbered *liniya* —Russian for lines—mark where most of the canals were to have been built.

The hazards of travel to the mainland and the constant threat of raging floods also played a role in Peter's decision to abandon Vasilyevsky Island and move to the mainland. When both channels of the Neva froze in winter, the island was cut off from the rest of Russia except by foot across the ice. Walking across the ice, in fact, became the only sure way to cross the river safely.

Undeterred, Peter had commanded diplomats and his court to take up residence in his new capital in 1712. Early visitors to St. Petersburg saw a city chronically short of food, constantly threatened by floods, and occasionally ravaged by wolf packs from the bleak northern forests. In 1714 a soldier guarding the central foundry reportedly was torn to pieces and eaten on the spot by wolves. A year later, wolves were said to have devoured a woman in broad daylight on Vasilyevsky Island, not far from Prince Menshikov's palace. A foreign diplomat described life in St. Petersburg as something akin to "hand-to-mouth bivouacking." But the emperor, who frequently lived in a three-room log cabin and drank beer with his sailors, would have his way.

Using imported German, French, Italian, and Dutch

artisans, noble families were required to build "English-style" houses of beams, lath, and plaster, the size of the homes depending upon how many slaves were owned. Wooden houses sufficed for more than a thousand merchants who were forced to St. Petersburg. Peter even ordered eight thousand songbirds for a new aviary to complement the growing number of parks and formal gardens featuring geometric flower beds in the best traditions of France.

Over the years, a multitude of French, Italian, and English architects erected about five hundred imposing palaces and public buildings of various shades of blue, pale green, yellow, and red—all in the name of Peter and his successors, their lovers, relatives, and patrons. Baroque gave way to classicism in architectural style under a building boom inspired by Empress Catherine II, the sharp-witted former German princess who married into the Romanov clan and became known as Catherine the Great.

At the heart of the city was the headquarters of the Russian navy, the Admiralty, topped with a 238-foot (72.5-meter) needlelike golden spire, with three wide avenues radiating from it. The flood-prone Neva was walled off by red-and-gray Finnish marble. Palatial mansions graced Nevsky Prospekt, the city's main thoroughfare, and its four great Venetian-like waterways, the Moika and Fontanka rivers and Catherine and Obvodny canals. Suspension bridges of intricate design linked islands studded with marble obelisks, Egyptian sphinxes, and cathedrals with spires more Western Catholic than Russian Orthodox.

By the nineteenth century, when St. Petersburg was in full bloom, enthusiasts called the glamorous capital the "Venice of the North"—a comparison earlier made popular by Peter himself. Today, the two cities certainly have one thing in common: the constant threat of floods that ravage the great cultural landmarks on both the Baltic and Adriatic seas. Grigory Kaganov, an architectural historian, has studied the myths of

THE ANGULAR RAMPARTS *of Peter and Paul Fortress (facing page), formed the nucleus of early St. Petersburg. In the distance stretch Vasilyevsky Island and the Gulf of Finland. St. Petersburg grew from a rough frontier outpost into a European capital of sweeping facades and elegant baroque and neoclassical buildings.*

THE
COLD
GRANITE
*ramparts
of the Peter and
Paul Fortress rise
beside the silent
Neva River, as it
finishes its short
46-mile-long
(74 kilometers) race
from Lake Ladoga
to the nearby Gulf
of Finland. Inside
the fortress, a
cannon near the
Saints Peter and
Paul Cathedral
booms every day
at noon, a custom
that goes back to
the eighteenth cen-
tury. In Peter's
time, Petersburgers
had to walk across
the ice in winter to
traverse the Neva,
for there were no
bridges until 1727.*

LEGEND SAYS *sailors bid farewell to their loved ones from
the Potseluyev, or "Kissing Bridge," in the old shipbuilding quarter of
New Holland, where the Moika River and the Kryukov Canal intersect
(above). St. Petersburg has about five hundred bridges that connect forty-
two islands, which are surrounded and intersected by eighty-six rivers,
streams, and canals. Two of the most picturesque waterways are the
Griboyedov or Catherine Canal (right) and the Winter Canal (far right).*

this "Venice of the North." He explains: "By the end of the eighteenth century, Russia's finest artists started to depict Petersburg using the Venetian style and image. But a century later, artists and writers didn't refer so much to canals, but to Petersburg's narrow dark streets, the whole Venetian facade, in comparing it to Venice. The finest representatives of the St. Petersburg intelligentsia saw themselves as Venetian. Life in Petersburg by the early twentieth century was a continuation of the Venetian carnival with Venetian masks much in vogue at court balls. The canals were largely forgotten." Some covered gondolas like those of Venice, however, did appear on Petersburg's canals as the city grew into a European capital. But, says Kaganov, Petersburg's gondolas were never more than a means of mass transit for the armies of civil servants who staffed the ministries of an empire.

REVIVING THE
CITY'S *imperial past, actors portray Peter the Great, his wife Catherine I, and their court to celebrate the birthday of Russia's second largest city and former imperial capital.*

Unlike other capitals built expressly for the business of government—upstart cities such as Washington, D.C.; Canberra, Australia; or Brasilia, Brazil —St. Petersburg owes its existence to forced labor and coercion. From across his empire, Tsar Peter summoned carpenters, stonecutters, masons, and laborers to build his capital. They lived in crowded and filthy huts, toiled in swamps and bogs, and died in droves from malaria, scurvy, and dysentery. In Peter's day somewhere between 40,000 and 100,000 Russian peasants and Swedish prisoners-of-war perished while building St. Petersburg. Petersburgers would speak for generations of "psychic energy" radiating from the corpses that, literally, made up the city's early foundation. To this day, Russians call St. Petersburg "a city built on bones."

METROPOLITAN ST. PETERSBURG

1. *Peter and Paul Fortress*
2. *Admiralty*
3. *Palace Square*
4. *Winter Palace/State Hermitage Museum*
5. *Strelka*
6. *Kuntskammer*
7. *Academy of Sciences*
8. *St. Petersburg State University*
9. *Art Academy*
10. *Russian Museum*
11. *Summer Garden*
12. *Engineer (St. Michael) Castle*
13. *St. Isaac's Cathedral*
14. *Kazan Cathedral*
15. *Beloselsky-Belozersky Palace*
16. *Alexander Nevsky Monastery*
17. *Smolny Institute*
18. *Cathedral of the Transfiguration*
19. *Mariinsky Theatre*
20. *Church of the Resurrection*
21. *Cruiser Aurora*
22. *Finland Station*
23. *Moscow Station*
24. *St. Nicholas Cathedral*
25. *Sennaya (Haymarket) Square*
26. *St. Petersburg Commodities and Stock Exchange*
27. *Kirov Stadium*
28. *Piskaryovskoye Cemetary*
29. *Baltic Shipyard*
30. *Admiralty Shipyard*
31. *Commercial Seaport*

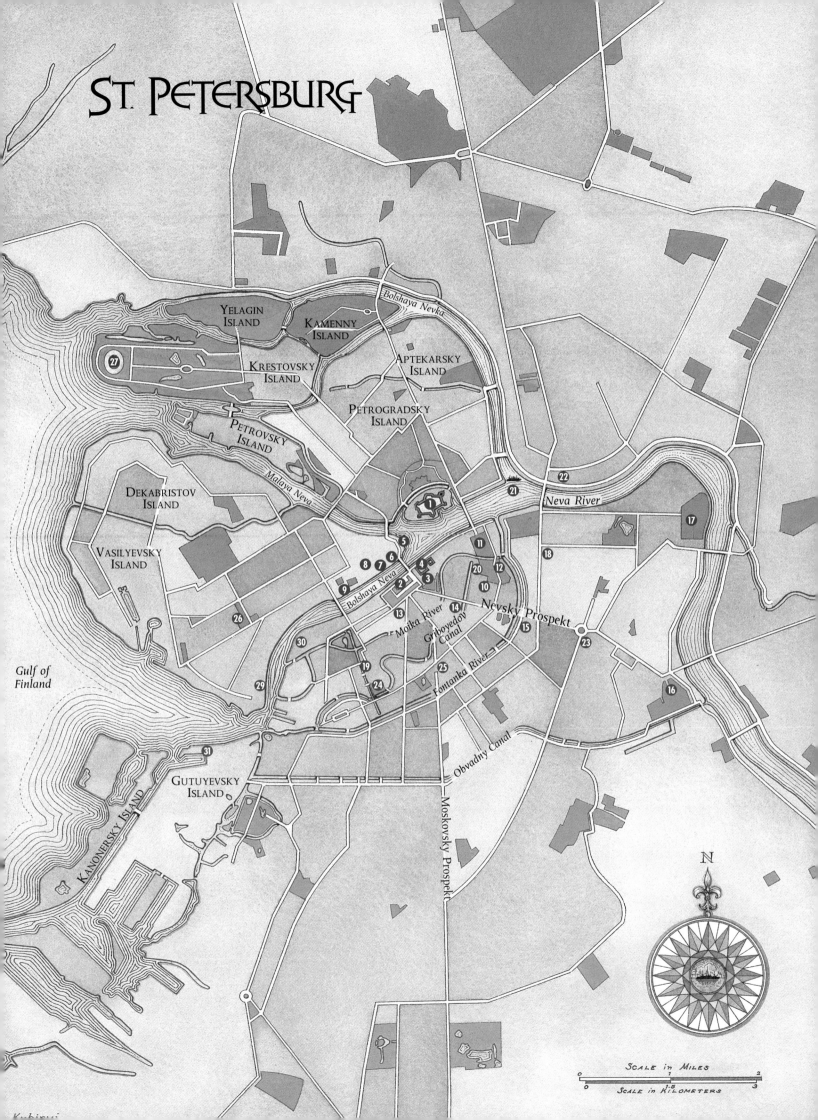

St. Petersburg

YELAGIN ISLAND

KAMENNY ISLAND

Bolshaya Nevka

KRESTOVSKY ISLAND

APTEKARSKY ISLAND

PETROGRADSKY ISLAND

PETROVSKY ISLAND

DEKABRISTOV ISLAND

Malaya Neva

VASILYEVSKY ISLAND

Bolshaya Neva

Neva River

Moika River

Griboyedov Canal

Nevsky Prospekt

Fontanka River

Gulf of Finland

Obvodny Canal

Moskovsky Prospekt

KANONERSKY ISLAND

GUTUYEVSKY ISLAND

N

SCALE IN MILES

SCALE IN KILOMETERS

SEARCHING FOR
*their Russian roots, history
enthusiasts dressed in the early
nineteenth-century uniforms of the
Pavlovsk Grenadiers (left) add an
authentic touch to an exhibition at
the St. Michael Castle, once a military engineering school. Trumpet
fanfare accompanies costumed
actors (above) to inaugurate St.
Petersburg's birthday celebration.*

"The curse of St. Petersburg is essential to understanding the city today," says Professor Jacob Gilinsky, a sociologist in the Russian Academy of Sciences who has followed the city's trends in suicide, drug addiction, and divorce for more than two decades. "Stalin also built cities with forced labor," says Gilinsky, "but no city has suffered more than St. Petersburg. First there were the tsars, then the Bolsheviks and the Nazis. It is part of our collective Russian mythology that this is the capital of misfortune—the city of the damned."

After Peter died in 1725, a series of high-spirited empresses spent the rest of the eighteenth century building an extravagant capital of stone, gold spires, and painted facades. Between 1801 and 1825, Tsar Aleksandr I, determined to make St. Petersburg the most exalted capital in Europe, added the finishing touches to the building boom Peter had started a century before. Architectural historians say that during the 1820s and 1830s, only the United States matched Russia in erecting so many public buildings of granite and marble, boasting great columns and triumphal arches —the neoclassical style so favored by Aleksandr I. In St. Petersburg, these projects included the Senate and Synod buildings, the semicircular General Staff Headquarters opposite the Winter Palace, and Kazan Cathedral on Nevsky Prospekt. Aleksandr I's crowning achievement, however, was St. Isaac's Cathedral, which took more than forty years to build.

But for people who thrive on raw emotion and tradition, Russians say St. Petersburg just isn't Russian. Architectural temples such as St. Isaac's share a common heritage with Rome, not the spiraling towers and onion domes of Moscow's ancient Kremlin fortress. And the delicate pastels of St. Petersburg's facades are more reminiscent of the Mediterranean than the Baltic.

Over the years, Russians have not been alone in their discomfort.

In 1839, Marquis de Custine, a French nobleman, traveled the Russian empire and found St. Petersburg full of pretension, especially in its architecture and art. He wrote: "I do not reproach the Russians for being what they are. What I blame in them is their pretending to be what we are. They are still uncultivated. . . .

I see them incessantly occupied with the desire of mimicking other nations, and this they do after the true manner of monkeys, caricaturing what they copy." The marquis saw in St. Petersburg not the collected glories of Western civilization—great sculpture, soaring churches, grand boulevards, new institutions of higher learning brimming with creativity—but a "camp of granite."

To the city's detractors, St. Petersburg would always be a "Babylon of the Snows," where the rich wallowed in carnal excess, the poor went hungry, and free expression was ruthlessly suppressed. It was a city more European than Russian, and Russian writers found themselves inventing a world of the supernatural to explain St. Petersburg. Fyodor Dostoyevsky and Nikolai Gogol

A F E A S T *of wedding-cake-like baroque decoration, the Nakhimov Naval School (facing page) trains high-school-age cadets in the traditions of the Russian fleet. The domes of St. Nicholas Cathedral (above), which is named for the patron saint of seafarers, and the great dome of St. Isaac's Cathedral capture the northern sunlight.*

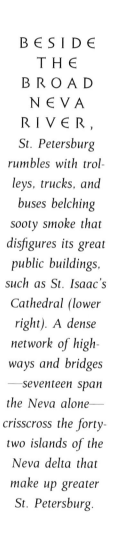

BESIDE
THE
BROAD
NEVA
RIVER,
St. Petersburg rumbles with trolleys, trucks, and buses belching sooty smoke that disfigures its great public buildings, such as St. Isaac's Cathedral (lower right). A dense network of highways and bridges —seventeen span the Neva alone— crisscross the forty-two islands of the Neva delta that make up greater St. Petersburg.

chronicled St. Petersburg's pretensions and bawdiness, while championing a vast underclass that worked the city's factories and filled its poorhouses and orphanages.

Gogol wrote of a St. Petersburg full of apparitions and otherwordly powers, a place where an overcoat could assume human qualities and "everything is full of deceit" on Nevsky Prospekt, the city's main street. For on Nevsky, he said, "the devil himself lights all the street lamps to show everything in anything but its true colors." And Gogol never reconciled himself to so Western a city populated by Slavs imitating Europeans. He likened St. Petersburg to a dandy preening before the mirrors of the Neva and Gulf of Finland, always "dressed and sauntering on the border." Gogol compared St. Petersburg to a "European-American colony," a city fractured by class and nationality more like the London of Charles Dickens than the Paris of Honoré de Balzac.

Dostoyevsky called living in St. Petersburg a "double misfortune," labeling it the "most abstract and premeditated city in the world." He probed the dark-

AN ALPINE CLIMBER *scales the dome of Kazan Cathedral, which is undergoing a facelift. Turned into a Communist "Museum of Religion and Atheism" in 1932, the cathedral is again open for weekly services. The cadences of the Orthodox liturgy soar 233 feet (71 meters) high in its dome. The cathedral—built between 1801 and 1811—remains a prominent Nevsky Prospekt landmark. At this and other St. Petersburg monuments, climbers are brought in to restore delicate paintings without the use of unsightly scaffolding.*

TSAR NICHOLAS II *(below) opens the first Russian parliament, called the Duma, on May 10, 1906, in the Winter Palace.
The short-lived experiment in a constitutional monarchy, called partially
in response to Russia's disastrous war with Japan and a bloody political
upheaval in St. Petersburg in 1905, failed to resolve Russia's massive
social ills. Orphans (facing page) eat a simple lunch of kasha, or boiled
cereal, reflecting the ever-widening gap between rich and poor that
haunted the final years of the Romanov dynasty and helped bring
about its downfall by Lenin's Bolsheviks.*

ness of St. Petersburg as often as he probed the darkness of the Russian mind. In the jumble of streets near Haymarket Square, where peddlers mixed with prostitutes and criminals, Dostoyevsky dodged his creditors. To pay his debts, he dashed off stories that smell of vodka, whores, blackmail, and murder. Rodion Raskolnikov, the crazed ax-murderer of an old woman in *Crime and Punishment*, lived in an attic here. Surveying the tracts of seedy apartment buildings that surround Haymarket Square today, now littered with discarded hypodermic needles and empty vodka bottles, a Russian literary scholar suggests that little has changed since Dostoyevsky's time. "Only Russians and alcoholics understand Dostoyevsky," says Bella Rybalko, director of the Dostoyevsky Museum.

Driven to make Russia a world power, Tsar Peter sparked an era that not only would produce world-class warships and cannon but also would result in a torrent of creativity in art, literature, drama, and politics over the next two centuries. At the same time, the sciences born in St. Petersburg would have far-reaching consequences in the world of physics, mathematics, botany, genetics, and psychology.

To train his engineers, shipwrights, and future generals, Peter created Russia's first academies staffed by European professors. He started the country's first public libraries and instituted a table of rank for military and civil servants based on education and merit. Rationalism was seen as a military necessity in order to foster the science, engineering, and technology need-

ed to support a world-class army and navy. By placing secular knowledge over spiritual belief, Peter brought the Russian Orthodox clergy to heel and established himself as the final arbiter of social needs. On University Embankment, Peter built his *Kunstkammer*, Russia's first museum—one devoted to "rarities, curiosities, and monsters," as the tsar saw it, collected on his many trips abroad. Even today it remains full of pickled mutants like Siamese twins, a two-faced man, and enough specimens of contorted and malformed animals to inspire a horror film.

It was in Peter's Kunstkammer that Mikhail Lomonosov founded the Russian Academy of Sciences, an institution that would nurture generations of scientists and Nobel laureates. A Russian version of Benjamin Franklin, Lomonosov was an accomplished chemist, physicist, geologist, metallurgist, historian, poet, and astronomer. He was far ahead of his time, especially in Russia, where science had no following and only one patron—Tsar Peter. Lomonosov worked long into the night in the fifth-floor dome of the Kunstkammer, gazing at the stars in Russia's first observatory, writing verse and history, codifying the rules of Russian grammar, and developing the science of physical chemistry.

Later, St. Petersburg would reign in the arts. Peter Tchaikovsky, a graduate of the city's music conservatory, was inspired here to write *Swan Lake*, *The Nutcracker*, and *Sleeping Beauty* for the Imperial Ballet, which went on to world fame as the Kirov. And a former naval lieutenant who taught himself to write music at sea, Nikolai Rimsky-Korsakov, thrilled audiences at

the St. Petersburg Symphony with melodies full of the pageantry of imperial Russia. Another ex-military officer, Modest Mussorgsky, wrote the symphonic poem *Pictures at an Exhibition* and the opera *Boris Godunov*, some of the most inspired music of the age. With fellow composers Borodin, Balakirev, Cui, and Rimsky-Korsakov, Mussorgsky joined the ranks of St. Petersburg's "Mighty Handful" who looked to their Russian roots, not the West, for inspiration.

A student named Marc Chagall, the product of a mystic and devout Jewish family, arrived in St. Petersburg in 1907 and changed the way the world looked at stained glass, sculpture, and modern painting. Chagall's time in St. Petersburg was a period of such accomplishment in the arts and sciences that it became known as the Silver Age or the Russian Renaissance. Russians excelled in modernist painting, ballet, and theatrical and operatic production. Bookstores overflowed with a public so enthusiastic that authors were able to afford estates. The poet Aleksandr Blok, a St. Petersburg fixture, earned five gold rubles a line, a fortune at the time.

One of Russia's greatest poets of the twentieth century, Anna Akhmatova started writing verse during

BELLA RYBALKO, *director of the Dostoyevsky Museum, surveys an attic room (above) where Raskolnikov, the crazed student murderer in* Crime and Punishment, *Dostoyevsky's novel of nineteenth-century psychological intrigue, may have lived. Not far from Haymarket Square, where social injustices and poverty moved Dostoyevsky to write many of his classics, a beggar (below) confronts Western tourists. During the long years of tsarist repression, the prison cells of the Peter and Paul Fortress (facing page) housed political dissidents, including Dostoyevsky and other famous Russian writers.*

those glittering years that coincided with the reign of Tsar Nicholas II, from 1894 to 1917. Her words mirrored the city's transformation from an imperial capital to the crucible of a lethal dictatorship.

"The dark city on the terrible river was my blessed cradle," wrote Akhmatova in one of her early love poems to St. Petersburg. Akhmatova never lost her affection for her birthplace, even when the Bolshevik commissars of Petrograd turned against her, declaring her a whore and banishing her poetry for a generation.

On November 8, 1917, a balding revolutionary named Lenin stepped to the platform at the Smolny Institute, an elite finishing school for girls in St. Petersburg, and quietly uttered words that would become catechism for the next seventy years: "We will now proceed to construct the Socialist order." Lenin's revolt in St. Petersburg transformed Russia into a colossus called the Soviet Union, gave the world its first Communist government, and cast the die for a global rivalry that came to be called the Cold War.

Lenin and his successors, determined to undo the tsarist regime, managed to perpetuate one dark legacy of the tsars—the suffering of St. Petersburg. Since Peter's day, those who challenged the divine right of the Romanovs to rule were brutally suppressed. The tsarist secret police also dealt harshly with freethinkers and radicals individually—Dostoyevsky was exiled to a Siberian prison in Omsk for four years. But Lenin and Soviet dictator Joseph Stalin decimated the St. Petersburg intelligentsia. As the Bolsheviks consolidated power, their thugs murdered, imprisoned, or exiled the city's intellectuals, artists, writers, musicians, composers, and surviving nobility—only a few survived the brutal purges of the 1930s and 1940s.

Composer Dmitry Shostakovich, a native son and graduate of the Petrograd music conservatory, was one of the lucky. He churned out a succession of sym-

DURING A FAILED ATTEMPT
to seize power from the interim government that followed Nicholas II, revolutionaries flee under fire in July 1917 on Nevsky Prospekt.

phonies through the dark years of war and repression, including his Seventh Symphony, the *Leningrad*, full of anger and defiance. His music became a rallying cry for a city besieged by the Nazis, and this public support may have spared him the fate of the poets Blok and Mandelstam and so many more. Wrote Shostakovich in his memoirs: "When I started going over the life stories of my friends and acquaintances, I was horrified. . . . Some came to a terrible end, some died in terrible suffering. . . . I was remembering my friends and all I saw was corpses, mountains of corpses." Shostakovich died in 1975, at a loss to explain how he survived when most of the artists of St. Petersburg's Silver Age committed suicide, fled abroad, or were ruthlessly murdered or imprisoned. "There was only one question of life or death," wrote Shostakovich. "How did the leader [Stalin] like your opus?"

Nazi armies encircled Leningrad in September 1941, beginning an epic nine-hundred-day siege that virtually cut off Russia's second largest city from the rest of the world until January 1944. Nearly three million Leningraders endured it; just under half of them died, starving or freezing to death. Leningrad's wartime losses would equal the total number of U.S. combat deaths

A RUSSIAN MILITARY BAND,
backed by the red flags of Communist diehards, mark the fiftieth anniversary of the lifting of the siege of Leningrad at Piskaryovskoye Cemetery, where some 800,000 civilians lie buried in mass graves.
The Communists and their sympathizers consider the cemetery sacred ground, since the battle for Leningrad was hard-won under the Communist rule.

in all of America's wars from the Revolution through Vietnam.

How many Leningraders really died in the siege? Careful calculations may be inexact by several hundred thousand. Official figures released after the war say 671,635 civilians died—641,803 from starvation alone. But Russian and Western historians believe the true figure exceeds one million. Their evidence is drawn from a calculation of how many bodies mass graves could hold: 800,000 bodies at Piskaryovskoye Cemetery and another 300,000 at Serafimov Cemetery. When the deaths of soldiers defending Leningrad are added to these figures, they total between 1.3 and 1.5 million persons.

Carrying flowers and memories, Russians trudge the ice-covered paths of winter to Piskaryovskoye Memorial Cemetery on the city's northeastern edge. An eternal flame flickers above mass graves marked starkly "1941," "1942," "1943," and "1944." The adagio lamentoso of a Tchaikovsky symphony hangs in the winter air, and a military honor guard braces at attention, eyes fixed on a forest of common graves among the birch trees. Before them stands Nina Umova, frail and bent but full of dignity, holding a sprig of paper violets close to her breast. Umova was twenty-nine years old on January 18, 1943—the day the Red Army punched through German lines, though fighting around Leningrad would continue for another year. Now, fifty years later, she has returned to Piskaryovskoye with thousands of other blockade survivors to remember that day of rejoicing—that day when red flags went up everywhere and citizens

danced down Nevsky Prospekt. Perhaps, too, she has come to say farewell once more to those who perished.

"I had to come; I must remember one more time," says Umova, who worked at the Karl Marx Factory making Katyushya multi-barreled rocket launchers during the siege. Umova was the only member of her family to stay behind in Leningrad during the war. Her loved ones, like thousands of Leningraders, were evacuated to Magnitogorsk and other cities in the distant Urals. "I was glad I didn't have to see them suffer," she says. "Too many suffered."

Suffering and remembering—this is what Piskaryovskoye is all about. A bronze statue called *Motherland* towers over the crowd of young and old gathered to celebrate the anniversary of the end of the siege. On a granite wall, overlooking the hundreds of thousands of intertwined dead, is an epitaph by Leningrad poet Olga Bergholz, another survivor. Chiseled for all time, it reads:

Here lie the people of Leningrad,
Here are the citizens—men, women, and children—
And beside them the soldiers of the Red Army
Who gave their lives
Defending you, Leningrad,
Cradle of Revolution.
We cannot number the noble
Ones who lie beneath the eternal granite,
But of those honored by this stone
Let no one forget, let nothing be forgotten.

THOUSANDS UPON THOUSANDS
of Leningraders rest in rows of mass graves at Piskaryovskoye Cemetery
(above), where the dead are identified only by the year they fell or suc-
cumbed to starvation during a nine-hundred-day siege by an encircling
Nazi army. A mourner (facing page) at Piskaryovskoye recalls the price
Leningrad paid for withstanding Hitler's onslaught. Hitler gave the city
its defining moment—no city lost more people than Leningrad, which
suffered more than one and a half million wartime deaths.

Memories of the siege seem fresh, even five decades later. At Number 14 Nevsky Prospekt on the city's main thoroughfare, a blue-and-white sign in Russian has been preserved as evidence of the punishing Nazi bombardment. It reads: "Citizens. During the shelling, this side of the street is the most dangerous." Gathered before the freshly touched-up sign, a band of retired World War II navy veterans plays spirited marches, and passersby, normally in a great hurry on the way to Nevsky's shops or bus stops, pause to talk with survivors of the siege.

"I don't like to talk about it much," says a tearful Yuri Komarov, a trainer at a St. Petersburg health club. "What you can find in a garbage dump today is better than what we ate." He confirms what many have written: that families boiled the leather covers of books to make a weak tea, while others ate rats, cats, or dogs until these too disappeared during the winter of 1941–42, the coldest on record in this century. Some resorted to cannibalism. A local politician, Vice-Mayor Pavel Novikov, speaks for many, including the young. He says: "Even though the citizens of Leningrad had nothing left to burn for heat, they kept a fire alive in their hearts. The younger generation bows down before you, who kept the city alive."

Leningrad survived the Nazis, but later, thousands more fell victim to rulers in the Kremlin. The civilian wartime death toll in Leningrad had called into question both Stalin's leadership and the generalship of the Red Army, so Stalin ordered history rewritten, understating Leningrad's sacrifice and minimizing its deaths. A city

museum devoted to the defense of Leningrad was closed, the blue-and-white notices warning of Nazi bombardment along Nevsky Prospekt were painted over, and a massive restoration effort was started to rebuild the great palaces and public buildings of the tsarist capital.

More of the city's writers and artists, plus scores of Communist Party politicians, were dispatched to Siberian labor camps or executed, lest they disclose the true scale of the tragedy. Massive numbers of war-wounded and prematurely retired workers also were sent to distant parts of the Soviet empire. New Party bosses considered these Leningraders a drag on the expanding economy and their high medical care costs an unnecessary expense. In their place came thousands upon thousands of workers, bureaucrats, students, and soldiers from every corner of the Soviet Union. Thus was Leningrad repopulated.

Between Stalin's death in 1953 and the fall of Communism in 1991, the long years of the Cold War turned Leningrad into the high-tech arsenal of the Soviet Union. Behind the facade of palaces restored down to the last piece of bric-a-brac, Leningrad became a top-secret outpost of the military-industrial complex. Assembly lines and design bureaus turned out micro-electronics, semiconductors, jet engines, atomic reactors, nuclear submarines, spy satellites, naval guns, and heavy tanks. Beneath the Aleksandr Nevsky Monastery, a secret navy research center tested submarine hulls that were made of steel and titanium alloys. As much as 80 percent of Leningrad's labor

CROWDS GATHER *in front of Kazan Cathedral*
(facing page) on Nevsky Prospekt to mourn the 1918 murders of the last
tsar, Nicholas II, and his family. The Russian tricolor flag is adorned with
a double-headed eagle—the imperial insignia. Praying for the soul of
Tsar Nicholas II, monarchists (above) seek a strong authoritarian
government in the Russian tradition. The last of the royal Romanov line,
a Frenchman, died in 1992 in Miami and was buried in the
Saints Peter and Paul Cathedral.

force and 75 percent of its industrial production were devoted to just one customer, the Soviet military.

Today, as Russia weaves unevenly toward democratic institutions and a market economy, St. Petersburg is taking a cue from its founding father. As Tsar Peter did almost three hundred years ago, the city—sixth largest in Europe—has thrown open its windows to breezes blowing from every direction, especially the West.

"We need to take off our armor and turn our face to the West once again," says Valentin Nazarov, director of the city's Masterplan Institute, a government agency charged with charting growth. "We need to rebuild our ties with Europe, America, and Japan." Nazarov's priorities—and the city's—include improvements in transportation, communications, and com- merce that would anchor St. Petersburg once and for all in the orbit of the industrialized democracies.

"Conversion from military production is the biggest problem facing St. Petersburg," says city planner Nazarov. "The fate of the city depends on how well the conversion process works. But no one can give you a recipe for it."

In the dark of winter, when the sun only peeks above the crimson-hued clouds of the eastern Baltic, St. Petersburgers shiver and think of their next meal. The food shortages that prompted international humanitarian aid in 1991 and 1992 have given way to a relative abundance of food but prohibitive prices caused by skyrocketing inflation. That most of the high-priced goods are Western imports has fueled growing anti-Western sentiment.

Die-hard Communists, more comfortable with the West as a Cold War enemy than as a friend and partner, rail against kiosks selling Old Milwaukee-brand beer and Western-made jogging shoes. Communists and ultra-nationalists, who have gathered strength under the infamous politician Vladimir Zhirinovsky, carry on a tradition of xenophobia that has run deep in the Russian character for a thousand years.

Occasionally their anger spills into the streets.

Nationalism in St. Petersburg has varied forms. Monarchists solemnly carrying blessed icons and images of Nicholas II turn out to demand a restoration of the House of Romanov and an end to Western-style government. Descendants of Cossacks have formed their own alliance to preserve Russian military, social, and cultural values. Fabled as the tsar's fierce warriors on horseback, Cossacks say their mission now is to defend Russian interests and honor against an onslaught of Western commercialism at home and anti-Russian sentiment in the shattered Soviet empire.

"We are carrying the banner for the salvation of Russia," claims Boris Almazov, ataman (leader) of the Nevsky Cossack regiment. "We are fighting the disease of Western influences and, with God's help, will restore Russian values." A literature professor and former military officer, Almazov recalls proudly that "Cossacks have been in Petersburg since the birth of the city. They rode with Peter the Great."

Extremist groups, though, find few true allies. Most Petersburgers are too busy putting food on the table or protecting their jobs at a time of rising unemployment to give the disgruntled more than a passing nod on Nevsky Prospekt, where fringe groups often gather to hawk hate-filled newspapers or hold vigils for a return to rule by the tsars.

"The monarchists today are just a curiosity," says Dmitry Likhachev, who recalls the days when Cossacks in bearskin caps rode at the head of Tsar Nicholas II's motorcade. "The monarchy had its own structures during imperial times and everything made sense. You could find a Russian monarch today, but nothing would come of it. Putting on a uniform doesn't change anything."

The only true monarch is St. Petersburg herself. She reigns like a dowager empress, retaining her European charm, her grace, and her mystique, while trying not to show her age. Exquisite facelifts called "restoration" are now commonplace and continual, even in these times of rampaging inflation and unfathomable budget deficits. The display is for the armies of Russians and international visitors alike who now besiege its palaces, parks, churches, museums, and concert halls.

Rechristened, St. Petersburg today is a city rediscovered, a city determined to celebrate its grandeur while coming to terms with its past. For all of its shortcomings, the city of Peter's creation remains home to Russians who have been more willing over the generations to embrace the West and its values than have their compatriots of the vast Eurasian interior. From the ballet to the stock market, from the research laboratories to rock music clubs, St. Petersburg remains Russia's window to the West.

A RUSSIAN ORTHODOX PRIEST (above) sprinkles holy water on the gleaming sabers of Cossack officers. St. Petersburg Cossacks take an impassioned oath to defend the "inviolability of the borders of the fatherland and the honor of Russia, not sparing my life." A retired colonel (facing page) and member of the Nevsky regiment wears the uniform of his ancestors, the Kuban Cossacks from southern Russia.

"$\mathcal{E}$*very stone here is a chronicle*
Unto itself."

Mikhail Dudin
St. Petersburg native and Soviet poet

THE LIVING MUSEUM

Light from a luxuriant autumn sun, filtered by golden maples, dances about the Great Hall of Catherine Palace, one of a half-dozen castles and estates that ring the St. Petersburg suburbs. Like priceless crown jewels, the mansions are the ultimate dowry bequeathed by Tsar Peter the Great and his successors to Russia and the world. At Catherine Palace, gilded mirrors trimmed with arabesque carvings amplify the sun's rays, illuminating the largest ceiling painting in all of Europe. Appropriately titled *The Triumph of Russia*, the 9,086-square-foot (846-square-meter) colossus takes its subjects from Peter's many passions. For the painting, like St. Petersburg, glorifies Russia's victories in war and its achievements in art and science.

Indeed, the stately Catherine Palace in the suburb of Pushkin, formerly called *Tsarskoye Selo* or the "Tsar's village," is a peerless triumph of Russian decorative art. Nowhere is St. Petersburg's imperial heritage more stunningly preserved nor the massive reconstruction effort since World War II more evident than at Catherine, the main summer residence of the royal family until 1917. The palace, *Yekaterininsky Dvorets*, takes its name not from Empress Catherine the Great, as many think, but from the first of four high-spirited empresses to rule eighteenth-century Russia—Catherine I, the Lithuanian-born second wife of Tsar Peter. Here in 1717, she built a modest country house on a dairy farm once owned by Finns.

By the time Catherine's daughter Empress Elizabeth I finished building a memorial to her mother, the original sixteen-room stone dwelling was transformed into a rival of Versailles. Under the direction of the most famous architect of the day, an Italian named Bartolomeo Rastrelli, the edifice grew to two hundred rooms housed behind an elongated baroque facade of aqua,

THE BAROQUE *handiwork of Bartolomeo Rastrelli, the most famous of Catherine Palace's many architects, has been beautifully preserved in the stately drawing rooms and decorative facade.*

CHAPTER TWO

CATHERINE PARK,
*with its landscaped French and
English gardens and its assortment
of pavilions, monuments, pagodas,
and bridges, mixes baroque,
neoclassical, and Chinese
architectural styles. Gilded wrought-
iron gates (below), adorned with
the double-headed Russian eagle
and a crown, open on to
Catherine Palace.*

white, and gold that stretched 1,000 feet (306 meters). Empress Catherine II, known as Catherine the Great, the most powerful woman to rule Russia, left her mark, too, adding more rooms and an English park to the French formal gardens. She built an array of pavilions, including Chinese-style pagodas, monuments to her victories over the Turks, and a pyramid in honor of her favorite dogs.

Eventually, the palace and one hundred other structures on the estate surpassed all the other royal residences of Russia in size and splendor. Here treaties were signed and ambassadors received. Much as Peter had intended when he built St. Petersburg, foreign visitors calling on Catherine the Great saw a display of wealth so overwhelming that there could be no doubt Russia had finally arrived as a world power.

Two centuries later, those riches regularly draw more than a million visitors a year to Catherine Palace and Park about 16 miles (25 kilometers) south of St. Petersburg. Millions more, including Russians who say they are fascinated by this part of their history largely imported from Europe, make pilgrimages to other nearby country residences: Peterhof or *Petrodvorets*, Peter the Great's sumptuous palace on the Gulf of Finland, and the Great Palace and Park at Pavlovsk. Less splendidly restored, but still handsome amid parks now overgrown and gone to seed, are the palaces at Lomonosov, sometimes called by its tsarist-era name *Oranienbaum*, and Gatchina.

At the Catherine Palace, the opulence and ostentation—rooms full of carved Baltic amber, silk tapestries, and more than twenty thousand objets d'art by craftsmen such as Chippendale and Fabergé—suggest why the Russian Revolution happened in the first place. But what is most astonishing is that Catherine Palace and Park Museum should still exist at all. Like many of St. Petersburg's nearly five hundred tsarist-era palaces, Catherine's mansion was reduced to ashes and broken timber during the bitter nine-hundred-day battle for Leningrad during World War II. The palace was caught in a no-man's-land during a murderous

AN EXQUISITE FACADE
and more than two hundred rooms display the baroque beauty of Catherine Palace.

VICTIM OF NAZI *vengeance, the Great Hall of Catherine Palace (above) was reduced to a charred shell during World War II. The mansion, including the Great Hall and the elaborately domed chapel (facing page), have been stunningly re-created, thanks mainly to a massive postwar restoration effort by the former Soviet government.*

artillery exchange between advancing Red Army and retreating Nazi troops. Once Soviet soldiers recaptured it, they had to disarm booby traps made from 2,200-pound (1,000-kilogram) bombs. Only then did the Russians discover the Nazis had looted the palace of its art treasures during the occupation.

Restoration of the building began in 1957 and eventually became the largest reconstruction project in all of Russia. The incredible inch-by-inch restoration of Catherine Palace has now reached the two-thirds mark, despite the economic crisis brought on by the collapse of the Soviet Union. Some thirty of the palace's fifty-eight main rooms have been completely rebuilt down to the last blue fireplace tile and crystal chandelier. The 1,500 acres (600 hectares) of parks and gardens are perfectly manicured by a staff of six hundred. The gilded State and Knights' dining rooms are laid with exquisite gold-etched china painted with scenes of

imperial Tsarskoye Selo and featherweight porcelains made in the 1760s. The walls of the Blue Chinese Drawing Room are upholstered with pagoda-etched silks, the Ante Choir Room with yellow silk woven with pheasants, peacocks, and other exotic birds. And the ornate baroque bedroom of Tsar Aleksandr I's wife, Elizabeth, is filled with a forest of fifty daintily decorated ceramic columns that run from floor to ceiling.

Behind the Great Hall of Catherine Palace, four modern-day Michelangelos are cloistered on a scaffolding three stories high above the ballroom's antechamber. Their painstaking job is to reconstruct a 4,800-square-foot (450-square-meter) ceiling painting called *Marriage of Bacchus and Ariadne* by Pietro and Francesco Gradichi, an Italian father and son who were popular artists in the middle of the eighteenth century. During World War II, when the palace was used as a barracks for Nazi soldiers, the entire ceiling

D E T A I L E D
C A R V I N G S *(above)*
mingle with gold-trimmed mirrors
in the Great Hall of Catherine
Palace. Catherine the Great, the
first foreign-born sovereign to rule
Russia, spared no expense decorat-
ing the palace, which takes its
name from Empress Catherine I,
wife of Peter the Great.

WORKING
FROM OLD
PHOTO-
GRAPHS
*and nineteenth-cen-
tury watercolors,
master craftsmen
Yuri Shitov, left,
and Boris Lebedev
have been working
eight years to
recreate the over-
sized masterpiece,*
Marriage of
Bacchus and
Ariadne. *The mas-
terpiece is part of
more than 21,500
square feet (2,000
square meters) of
ceiling paintings
they have restored
at Catherine
Palace, whose ceil-
ings cover a colos-
sal 48,450 square
feet (4,500 square
meters). They also
have helped renew
ceiling paintings at
St. Isaac's and
Kazan cathedrals,
the Hermitage
State Museum, and
the palaces of
Petrodvorets,
Gatchina, and
Lomonosov.*

was destroyed. The painters working today—all men in their sixties—are considered national art treasures themselves because their talents are so specialized and sought after. They spent four years just studying old photographs and watercolor paintings of the original ceiling and making a life-size sketch to use as a pattern. The actual painting, another four-year task, continues in a cramped studio atop the scaffolding.

"God grant them good health," says Nikolai Nagorsky, assistant director of the museum. "I hope to God they are able to finish their work," he continues, "because after them, there is no one. There isn't another generation of geniuses who know this craft." After redecorating palaces all over St. Petersburg and its suburbs, the artists already have restored more than 21,500 square feet (2,000 square meters) of ceilings at Catherine, including its sweeping Great Hall. "Even Michelangelo didn't work that hard," says Nagorsky.

Catherine Palace, like all of the suburban mansions, is now part of a special United Nations archi-

tectural protection zone. This distinction makes nearby development, especially Soviet-style concrete sprawl, more difficult. The United Nations Educational, Cultural, and Scientific Organization (UNESCO) also has placed the entire city center—about 7 percent of municipal St. Petersburg—on its World Heritage List, making a collective monument of the city's streets, canals, bridges, squares, and old buildings. Aided by UNESCO, the Russian government has compiled a list of St. Petersburg's Monuments of History and Culture, a distinction that theoretically thwarts using these landmarks for commercial purposes or destroying their facades.

Meanwhile, financially hard-pressed St. Petersburg has tentatively leased dozens of run-down historic buildings to scores of international investors and Russian firms that are willing to restore them. The move, which was justified by the city's property commission as the only way to save the crumbling legacy of the tsars, has sparked a storm of protest from Petersburgers fearful that American, West European, and Japanese businesses will soon own their down-

town. The leasing controversy, like the UN's interest in St. Petersburg, is recent. Until 1990, when UNESCO became active, restoration of the war-ravaged city depended upon the resources and muscle that Russia alone could muster.

That muster had become mandate even before World War II ended, when Leningrad became the first major Russian city to rebuild on a massive scale—a decision that had as much to do with preserving the Kremlin's totalitarian grip on the country as it did with restoring buildings and preserving a culture imported from Europe that many Communists despised. Soviet leaders were anxious to erase the scars of World War II, which left more than 60 percent of the city's official and historic buildings damaged and destroyed. The million-plus death toll and widespread

destruction to landmarks like Nevsky Prospekt, the Winter Palace, and St. Isaac's Cathedral raised questions about Stalin, the leadership of the Communist Party, and the high command of the Red Army.

Thus, the same party bosses who earlier sent thousands of the city's artists and aristocrats to Siberian death camps found themselves co-opted by preservationists anxious to rebuild the architectural treasures of imperial St. Petersburg. The calculation was crude: Cold War antagonists and Third World clients would be as easily dazzled by rebuilt palaces and restored churches as by the tank factories and Siberian dams that were regularly touted as proof of Soviet superiority. If the tsars could impress foreign visitors at places like Catherine Palace, the argument went, so could the Kremlin.

The job of rebuilding the city's landmarks fostered

IN 1944, *retreating Nazi troops set fire to the palace at Peterhof (left), which was designed to resemble the palace of Versailles. Advancing Russian troops found the emblem of Hitler's elite "SS" troops on the grounds of Aleksandr Palace at Pushkin (above). By the 1960s, most of the palaces and parks at Peterhof had been restored, including most of the 144 fountains and three cascades in Lower Park (below).*

A BLAZE OF AUTUMN COLOR
*surrounds the Temple of Friendship at Pavlovsk
Palace and Park. The estate's waterways and
promenades (preceding pages) are weekend
favorites with Petersburgers.*

a whole new industry—reconstruction. A generation of painters and sculptors learned the specialized skills of "monumental art" that European architects had perfected two centuries earlier. New bureaucracies spent millions of rubles that, because of the unreliability of Soviet-era statistics, an artificial exchange rate, and distortions of the Soviet economy, cannot be easily translated into dollars. The former Soviet Ministry of Culture said Leningrad alone commanded 20 percent of the post–World War II budget for restoration and preservation of historic landmarks for the entire Soviet Union. St. Petersburg's restoration appears so thorough that it looks as if World War II never happened. The historic city center could just as easily be the nineteenth-century city of Dostoyevsky and Tchaikovsky.

But St. Petersburg city officials and palace directors speak of their frustration and impatience with the slow pace of the restoration effort. Skilled workers are in short supply, in part because younger artists can make more money in private businesses. Many say Russia's headlong rush to embrace capitalism and make the U.S. dollar the country's de facto currency has only complicated their problems. Aleksandr Kobak, deputy director of the private St. Petersburg Cultural Fund, calls the dreams of many Petersburgers for a restoration boom fueled by tourist dollars and international investment "complete utopia." Returning the city to its imperial glory would require colossal amounts of capital, he says, spending that is

THE ROMANOV TSARS *reigned from gilded thrones, such as Emperor Paul I's in suburban Gatchina Palace (above). In St. Petersburg, ambassadors presenting their credentials used the Ambassadors' or Jordan Staircase at the Winter Palace (right). The staircase owes its name to the Jordan Festival—the Epiphany celebrated on January 6 by the Russian Orthodox Church. In imperial times, the royal family would descend the staircase to join the blessing of the nearby Neva.*

beyond the means of most rich countries, let alone bankrupt Russia.

And money for reconstruction—especially valuable foreign currency—is lost in a quagmire of competing local and national bureaucracies. Restoration projects are slowed or sidetracked by turf battles at a time when leases go to the highest, though not necessarily the most worthy, bidder. And while international companies and foundations have stepped forward with ambitious plans to renovate historic buildings and palaces, they are sometimes opposed by suspicious Petersburgers who feel humiliated by the country's seeming inability to solve its overwhelming problems without kowtowing to the West.

Polish workers hired to renovate the system of majestic hydraulic fountains at Petrodvorets walked off the job for two years following a Russian government decision to freeze foreign currency payments. Now Moscow has come up with $500,000 to resume work, and is spending another $1.5 million for the famous fountains—clogged by runoff from a nearby pig farm—to be turned on again.

City restoration managers are contemplating yet another colossal restoration effort for the Aleksandr Palace in Pushkin, a mansion of ramrod-straight classical lines that seems mismatched situated next to the Catherine's baroque opulence. For now, this project seems to be far in the future, and the palace's resident naval institution has not yet looked for other quarters.

Further afield, the meticulous restoration of Gatchina Palace, favorite retreat of Emperor Paul I, is finally under way in the wooded countryside 28 miles (45 kilometers) south of St. Petersburg. A secret nuclear research laboratory located nearby kept the estate off-limits to Western visitors until 1992. Today, Gatchina's fortified towers and its labyrinth of underground passageways give the palace the look of an overgrown medieval castle, not the palatial estate of a

A FAINT WINTER SUN
warms the swirling exterior of the Winter Palace (left), built between 1754 and 1762 along the Neva River by the architect Bartolomeo Rastrelli "solely for the glory of all Russia." Today the Winter Palace forms the heart of the State Hermitage Museum.

tsar. Inside, more than a half-dozen rooms have been restored, including Emperor Paul's Upper Throne Room, which overlooks parks and lakes that cover more than 1,700 acres (about 689 hectares). Made of thick limestone and considered virtually fireproof, Gatchina weathered World War II better than other royal residences—at least its exterior was left standing.

Gone, however, are the wall paintings and furniture with erotic motifs that decorated Gatchina when Empress Catherine the Great built it in 1781 for one of her many lovers, Count Grigory Orlov. The overall loss of paintings and decorative art is staggering. Of 220,000 objets d'art listed in a 1919 inventory of Gatchina, fewer than 15,000 survived a sales orgy by the cash-strapped Bolsheviks and a looting binge by the Nazis. Many of the pieces that were sold are now in Western museums or private collections.

The tsars may have preferred the splendor and isolation of the Catherine or Aleksandr palaces, but their official residence always remained the Winter Palace, Rastrelli's flamboyant baroque temple with Roman gods adorning the roof. The 1,057-room Winter Palace covers twenty acres between the Neva Embankment and Palace Square, where today horse-drawn carriages full of tourists clatter over cobblestones worn smooth by strutting Russian armies. The palace has survived fires, terrorist bombs, two revolutions, and numerous attacks by the Nazis, who listed it on German maps as "bombing objective number 9." And few places in Russian history are more famous for their excesses or, perhaps, more soaked in the blood of Russians who tried to challenge their rulers.

Inside the Winter Palace—the most extravagant

IRREPRESSIBLE MUSEUM GOERS,
Russians outnumber international visitors to the State Hermitage Museum, a treasure house best known for its colossal collection of fifteen thousand paintings. Beneath an Italian masterpiece (facing page), an elderly couple watch their time, while a pair of young viewers (top) are drawn to a gallery of 329 portraits of Russian military leaders who defeated Napoleon in 1812. Empress Catherine the Great (above) founded the Hermitage, though this statue resides in the rival State Russian Museum.

"I HAVE
a whole labyrinth
of rooms . . . and
all of them are
filled with luxu-
ries," wrote
Empress Catherine
the Great of the
Winter Palace and
Hermitage art gal-
leries. Pavilion
Hall in the Small
Hermitage dazzles
the eye with white
marble columns,
Moorish water
fountains, crystal
chandeliers, and a
floor of mosaic tile
patterned after
ancient Rome.

and extensive court in all of Europe—about six thousand people lived and worked in a fairyland of luxury built between 1754 and 1762 for Empress Elizabeth I, daughter of Peter the Great. Balls and receptions regularly drew crowds of five thousand guests, according to Suzanne Massie, an American author and an authority on St. Petersburg court life. Equerries in plumed hats and patent-leather slippers, Ethiopian servants in frock coats and pantaloons, and Cossack guards ready to give their lives to defend the tsar catered to every whim of emperors and empresses and their families, government ministers and officials, and ladies and gentlemen in waiting.

When Empress Catherine the Great lived in the Winter Palace (1762–96), historians say, the expensive French finery of Russian aristocrats was rarely matched by polite French manners. At the entrance to one hall,

the empress published ten rules on how to behave at lavish masked balls or in private meetings with her intimates like Voltaire. Visitors were commanded to leave their rank at the door along with hats and swords, to "banish sighs and yawns," and to "drink with moderation, that each may walk steadily as he goes out," lest they offend Catherine's Germanic sense of order.

In the shadow of this same palace in 1905, hundreds of workers were gunned down while trying to deliver a petition to Tsar Nicholas II, who was not even home at the time. The Bloody Sunday massacre —in which as many as two hundred unarmed, hymn-singing petitioners were killed and another eight hundred wounded—is remembered today as the first act of revolution that ultimately brought down

ON A QUIET DAY *at the Hermitage Museum, visitors can find themselves alone among masterpieces. A schoolgirl eyes da Vinci's* Madonna With a Flower *(left), a prize among the museum's treasurehouse of more than three million works of art and artifacts. Housed in four sprawling palaces, the Hermitage has about 140 rooms devoted to Western painting, including sixteen galleries for Italian masterpieces (facing page).*

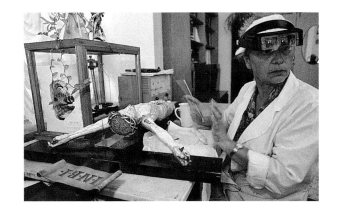

the Romanovs. On the night of October 25–26, 1917, Lenin's Bolsheviks stormed the palace, and in the White Dining Room they arrested the ministers of Aleksandr Kerensky's provisional government—a weak and short-lived parliamentary regime that had forced Nicholas II's abdication nine months earlier.

Since the October Revolution, the Winter Palace has formed the heart of the State Hermitage Museum. Comparable to the Louvre in Paris, the British Museum in London, and the Metropolitan Museum of Art in New York, the Hermitage comprises four sprawling palaces and today remains one of the world's great treasure-houses. The long years of Communist dictatorship, when Soviet authorities virtually sealed the country's borders and sanitized its press and broadcasting, only added to the Hermitage's importance. An oasis in a desert of propaganda, the museum was a place where ordinary Russians could learn about their cultural links to the rest of the world, especially the West.

Rooms full of marble, malachite, and jasper stir pride in a long-suffering Russian public that looks to the conquests and wealth of the tsars for a new sense of identity. And Russians thirsting to learn about Western religion, art, and culture surge to the Hermitage's picture galleries—140 rooms of which are devoted to Western painting alone. In front of Rembrandt's *Return of the Prodigal Son*, one of the Hermitage's most-prized masterpieces, a guide gives school children a stirring rendition of the New Testament story. For many, it is the first time they have heard one of Christianity's great parables.

Catherine the Great built the Small Hermitage in 1764 as a private art gallery, which adjoined the Winter Palace, to house the 225 canvasses she acquired in exchange for canceling a Berlin merchant's tax debt. But Catherine collected paintings by Rembrandt, Rubens, and Van Dyck at such a fast pace that she had to build a second pavilion, called the Large (or Old) Hermitage, twenty years later. Subsequent rulers built the Hermitage Theater and a New Hermitage, and Nicholas I opened them all to the intelligentsia, though not the general public, in 1852. The whole imperial collection, which today numbers about fifteen thousand paintings (including two Madonnas from the brush of Leonardo da Vinci), finally became public property after 1917.

Lenin's Bolsheviks added to the Hermitage's booty, confiscating enormous holdings of privately owned art. They forced two rich Moscow merchants to hand over what became one of the world's largest collections of French Impressionist and Early Modern paintings and divided the works of Gauguin, Cezanne, Monet, Renoir, Degas, Matisse, and Picasso between the Hermitage and Moscow's Pushkin Museum. Today the French Impressionist and Early Modern works, tucked away in eighteen rooms on the third floor of the Winter Palace, remain in demand for international exhibitions. This collection includes seven paintings by Van Gogh, eleven by Cezanne, fifteen by Gauguin, thirty-five by Matisse, and thirty-six by Picasso.

Renting out some of the Hermitage's art treasures is one way a new team of curators raises money to keep Russia's premier museum open and its collection of about three million artifacts intact. Officials have no intention of imitating the Bolsheviks, who sold off imperial art treasures to earn desperately needed foreign exchange. With some bitterness, curators and guides recount how American industrialist Andrew Mellon bought twenty-one paintings from the Hermitage—

WITH LESS THAN TEN PERCENT

of its artifacts on display at any one time, much of the Hermitage's collection is being restored in workshops that honeycomb the museum. Aleksandr Kuznetsov (above) clears away layers of paint added by other restorers to a sixteenth-century Dutch masterpiece. The gentle hands of chemist and art historian Klara Nikitina (facing page) clean an ivory crucifix from Germany.

SCORES OF SELDOM-SEEN STATUARY
*clutter Hermitage offices (above) and the crowded corridors of the Russian
Museum (facing page). St. Petersburg museums lack funds for facilities to
store their vast collections properly—or to display more than a fraction of
the cultural icons accumulated by the tsars and Soviet rulers. A thousand-
year history of Russian art, including the oversized canvasses of Karl
Briullov and Ilya Repin, is displayed in the Russian Museum.*

paintings that became the foundation of the National Gallery of Art in Washington, D.C.

"Exporting exhibits is definitely helping to offset our costs," explains Chief Curator Vladimir Matveyev, a specialist on the inventions of Peter the Great. "We already have mounted an exhibit on the life and times of Catherine the Great. It's gone to Memphis, Dallas, and Los Angeles. There will undoubtedly be more."

But forming partnerships with Western museums is only part of the job for the affable Matveyev, who once worked on a Siberian railroad and calls himself a jack-of-all-trades. Most days he is hunched over a French-made personal computer analyzing spreadsheets, ledgers, and inventory lists in a dingy office that seems too small for his portly frame. The problems seem constant and petty: How to pay the heating or electrical bills for the Hermitage's more than 350 often dark and cold halls that provide 13 miles (20 kilometers) of exhibition space? Where to store about twelve thousand pieces of sculpture, six hundred thousand works of graphic art, and one million coins and medals? Partly because the Hermitage is running out of space, less than 10 percent of the collection is on display at any one time.

There's more: How to fix the leaky roofs of the Winter Palace? How to pay for air conditioning that is being installed to protect Dutch Old Masters and French Impressionists from the dampness of St. Petersburg? Can the Hermitage afford to replace its outdated burglar alarm system? And what to do about some of the thirteen hundred staff members who always seem to be threatening to go on strike for higher pay? Matveyev takes little comfort from knowing these woes were considered trivial during the flush years of Communism, when the Soviet Ministry of Culture paid for the Hermitage's upkeep, acquisitions, and prodigious archaeological expeditions in Central Asia and the Middle East. Now the state will continue to foot only a fraction of the Hermitage's bills.

Directors of some of the city's more than ninety other museums—institutions that run the gamut from poet Anna Akhmatova's apartment to the zoo—say they are in worse shape. Only St. Petersburg's two superstars, the Hermitage and the State Russian Museum, have the bureaucratic clout in Moscow and the reputations abroad to plunge ahead, however awkwardly, with new exhibitions and acquisitions. The two giants already have fought a turf battle for control of the Marble Palace just a few blocks away from the Winter Palace. The fight is considered symbolic of the scramble for palaces that followed the collapse of Moscow bureaucracies into warring fiefdoms.

The overcrowded Russian Museum, housed in the neoclassical Michael Palace and an adjacent building specially built for the museum, won the tussle. The Marble Palace, formerly a branch of Moscow's Central Lenin Museum and full of busts of the founder of the Soviet state, has been turned into a national portrait gallery. But the Russian Museum did not stop with the Marble Palace, itself a neoclassical edifice built (for one of Catherine the Great's lovers) of thirty-two kinds of marble and considered extravagant even by St. Petersburg standards. The museum also has acquired palaces that showcase baroque and romantic architectural styles. With more than 350,000 objects in its collection, the Russian Museum is considered an encyclopedia of Russian art from twelfth-century icons to the giant canvasses of Kasimir Malevich, the darling of the early twentieth-century avant garde. Hounded

by the Bolsheviks, Malevich took refuge inside the Russian Museum on the Square of the Arts. Now the museum owns one hundred of his paintings—the largest Malevich collection in the world.

Restoration work already is under way at the Russian Museum's other acquisitions—the Stroganov Palace on Nevsky Prospekt and the *Mikhailovsky Zamok*, or the St. Michael Castle. Surrounded by moats and laced with secret passageways, the salmon-red St. Michael Castle became a military engineering school—and hence its nickname, the *Inzhenerny* or Engineer Castle—after the royal family gave it up when Emperor Paul I was murdered there in his bed in 1801 by conspirators. Dostoyevsky studied there from 1837 to 1843. Now Russian Museum officials are trying to evict two unwelcome tenants—the regional Center for Scientific and Technical Information and the

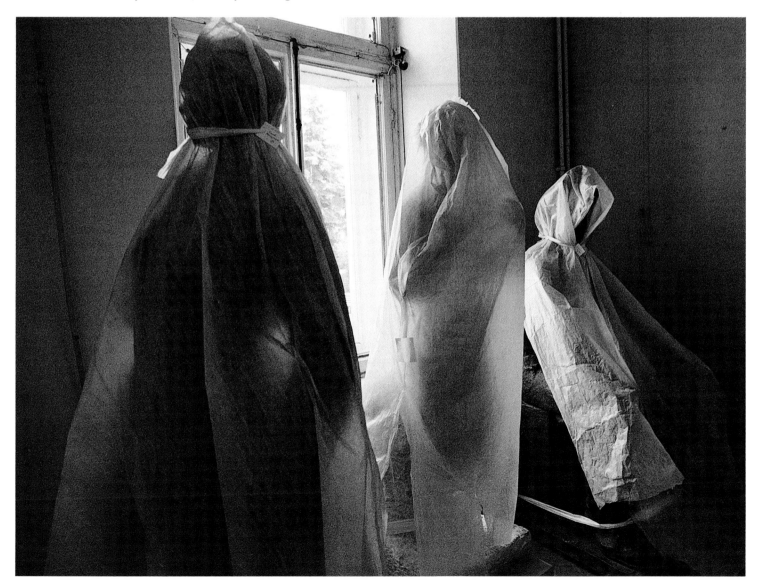

Central Naval Library—while moving ahead with restoration efforts financed largely by the Russian Ministry of Culture.

The Stroganov Palace, another of Rastrelli's pieces of baroque handiwork, was the stronghold of one of Russia's prominent families, a merchant clan that prospected the Urals under Ivan the Terrible and later patronized the arts and sciences until the Bolsheviks scattered them across Europe. The family coat of arms is still visible on the palace's Corinthian columns. A government agency designed to protect national monuments took over the Stroganov in 1987, but not before the disgruntled former tenants—a naval shipbuilding institute—vandalized it. Walls and floors were ripped up to cart out a massive computer and remove security and eavesdropping equipment. It will be years before the palace is open to an admiring public, though a Stroganov family foundation is helping with the job of restoring this and other St. Petersburg landmarks.

Such turmoil of the Russian cultural establishment helps explain why the Hermitage's Matveyev is seen in diplomatic drawing rooms and hotel lobbies as often as he is in the museum. With his boss, Mikhail Piotrovsky, a smooth Arabist and former university professor, Matveyev woos Western business and foundation executives to help underwrite some of the Hermitage's costs. And from all reports, their efforts are beginning to pay off. Coca-Cola, for example, is pairing a $50 million investment in a St. Petersburg soft drink plant with a $320,000 grant to the Hermitage. The grant money is being spent on a new high-tech laboratory to restore the tempera paintings of early Byzantine and Russian icons and early Italian and Spanish paintings.

Piotrovsky also created a Hermitage Foundation in the United States and tirelessly courted Western museum directors to help fund it. Some Petersburgers and international museum specialists credit Piotrovsky's astute fund-raising with the fact that he was born into the rarefied world of international museum circles. His father, Boris, enjoyed a worldwide reputation as an Egyptian scholar and as the feisty Hermitage director who battled both the Bolsheviks and the Nazis during a career that spanned seven decades. The elder Piotrovsky is credited with saving much of the Hermitage's collection during World War II by shipping priceless paintings and artifacts into the Ural Mountains, beyond the reach of German soldiers.

It was all the more ironic, then, when his son and the Hermitage stunned Western art enthusiasts in 1992

EMPEROR PAUL I *built St. Michael's Castle (facing page) at the intersection of the Moika and Fontanka rivers. More medieval fortress than castle, it failed to protect the tsar, who was murdered in his sleep forty days after he moved in on March 11, 1801. Now part of the Russian Museum, the stronghold once housed a military engineering school and counts Dostoyevsky among its earliest students. (detail, above)*

with an exhibition of art treasures looted by the Red Army from Germany's Bremen Museum at the end of World War II. The long-hidden collection of 138 drawings was found in storage in a Moscow museum and was transferred to the Hermitage for safekeeping and restoration. The booty includes works by Rembrandt, Van Dyck, Toulouse-Lautrec, Degas, Rodin, and Van Gogh, whose pencil sketch for *Starry Night,* drawn in 1888, had not been seen for more than fifty years. Matveyev says it is a matter for the Russian and German governments to decide if the art will be repatriated, and the Russian Ministry of Culture will only say that it is prepared to discuss ownership of the Bremen Collection in exchange for art treasures German soldiers took from Russia.

Like the Russian Museum, the Hermitage has expansion plans of its own. It has acquired part of its elegant next-door neighbor, the sweeping Russian Army General Staff Building on Palace Square, for a museum of applied arts. Just across the Neva, the Hermitage has claimed the palace of Prince Aleksandr Menshikov to exhibit eighteenth-century Russian art

and culture. Piotrovsky and Matveyev also have presided over the opening of the newly renovated Hermitage Theater, where ballet and opera performances are staged for select patrons. They hope to move some of the Hermitage's two hundred curators into new quarters, opening up more space in the Winter Palace for, among other things, a few rooms just to show how the royal family lived.

"The nobility is part of our Russian culture, part of our Russian heritage," says Matveyev, "and people want to know about it."

One of the purveyors of luxury to the royal family was the House of Fabergé, one of about twenty-five jewelers on *Bolshaya Morskaya* not far from the Winter Palace. Here the dynasty founded by Gustav Fabergé, of French Huguenot descent, crafted imaginative objects of pure fantasy under the warrant "Jeweler and Goldsmith to the Imperial Court." During the opulent nineteenth century, Fabergé's eldest son, Peter Carl, ran a staff of five hundred

people with shops in St. Petersburg, Moscow, Kiev, Odessa, and London. The St. Petersburg workshops alone turned out everything from the fifty-eight signature Fabergé Easter eggs to bracelets, cigarette boxes, picture frames, tea sets, and miniatures made of crystal, lapis lazuli, jasper, and agate.

But the Bolsheviks saw these as objects of tsarist conceit, not art. They nationalized the House of Fabergé in 1918, and Fabergé fled to France on ten minutes' notice, taking only his hat and coat. In fact, the Bolsheviks expropriated most of Bolshaya Morskaya, where the marquees of Cartier and Tiffany & Company competed with Fabergé. What had been known as the "street of gold" or "diamond row" became *Ulitsa Gertsena* in honor of Aleksandr Herzen, an early Russian revolutionary and theorist. By the 1930s, the struggling Soviet Union was so desperate for hard currency that Stalin sold most of the royal family's Fabergé trinkets to a few Western collectors, including the late Armand Hammer, the Los Angeles oil tycoon.

Now the four-storied, double-winged House of Fabergé at number 24 Bolshaya Morskaya is being restored by a determined group of Americans and Russians who want to help the city reclaim part of its noble past, when St. Petersburg was the jewelry-making center of the world. Officials of the private Fabergé Arts Foundation, one of several Western-backed

charitable groups active in St. Petersburg preservation circles, see its work as a harbinger for small-scale restoration projects that can help the city's faltering economy. Besides restoring the art nouveau building and turning it into a museum of imperial luxury, the foundation is creating an art center and workshops to showcase the Russian jewelry industry, which, to the surprise of many, still exists in St. Petersburg. "This isn't a project that is going to set the world on fire," explains Mary Ann Allin, one of the foundation directors. "But we think the entrepreneurial genius of Fabergé can be tapped to teach the marketing of the arts."

In post-Communist, free-enterprise St. Petersburg, conflicts over property ownership and money continue to confound both Western investors and Russian preservationists in the absence of an approved overall plan to redevelop the city's historic center. In 1991, city officials devised a plan to lease dozens of historic buildings to help pay for restoration and redevelopment work. But a $5 billion bid by the London-based European Bank for Reconstruction and Development for a fifty-year lease on four aging apartment buildings ignited a firestorm of protest. City council members voiced a common complaint, claiming officials were "giving away the city to for-

M A I N   S T R E E T *of the tsars, Nevsky Prospekt (in 1900, above, and today, facing page) remains St. Petersburg's most important thoroughfare. When it was completed in 1718, the street was called the Great Perspective Road, connecting the golden-spired Admiralty, center, to the Aleksandr Nevsky Monastery, a distance of 2.7 miles (4.5 kilometers).*

eigners." Meanwhile, buildings stand empty while politicians nurse their sense of wounded pride or their growing sense of humiliation at the hands of international bankers.

St. Petersburg's existing budget for historic preservation work also has been badly eroded by the precipitous drop in value of the Russian ruble, which has become nearly worthless during a time of runaway inflation. The city has enough money to cover the costs of repairing only a handful of tsarist-era buildings—a mere drop in the bucket compared to the ambitious plans of foreign developers, Western charitable foundations, and the St. Petersburg Commission on Architecture.

"The buildings are crumbling all around us from the war and seventy years of neglect," says Valery Yeggi, the commission's vice-chairman. "We're trying to resolve the problem using foreign investment, but it's not going so well." International investors say they are leery of unclear laws on property ownership and downright frightened by the continuing political instability in Russia. As one Western foundation adviser points out: "There are still no private property rights that any state bureaucracy respects."

At restored turn-of-the-century hotels that accept only Western currencies, international delegations, from both charitable foundations and private business, come and go like clockwork. But Western guests and their Russian hosts often express disappointment over misunderstood promises of help and still-born agreements to pay for improvements. Much seems to be lost in the translation—not in the words, but in the abrupt meeting of two cultures in which everything from tax

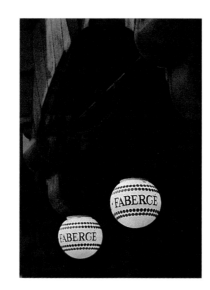

laws to gratuities seems contradictory. Even the term "charitable foundation" has a different meaning in dollar-hungry Russia. Western groups customarily see foundations as not-for-profit enterprises that are long on generosity and short on salaries and perquisites. Russian officials, however, generally expect only profits from foundations. Or, after brokering a deal with what looks like a reliable partner, preservationists are sometimes surprised when another government department—or a powerful Moscow bureaucracy—asserts ownership of a building or land. Sometimes the issue is money or who gets a share in the dollars being spent on rehabilitation.

The stickiest problem for potential investors remains a legal framework in Russia that is subject to constant revision and overlapping authority. When and if more coherent and effective property rights and tax laws are enforced, city officials think St. Petersburg could be modernized in less than a decade. So far, more than thirty shopping malls and office complexes are at various stages of planning, and some are gigantic in their size and ambition. For example, a Finnish company has offered to tear down a furniture factory and replace it with a futuristic business development. And Mayor Sobchak already has approved plans by a Dutch company to turn Dostoyevsky's old haunt, Haymarket Square, into a glass-encased shopping mall. As part of the $200-million deal, the company will rebuild the Uspensky Cathedral that was demolished in the early 1960s. But banks and investors willing to finance the developments demand property deeds before construction can begin.

THE WORKSHOPS *of world-renowned jeweler Peter Carl Fabergé, whose intricate creations catered to the whim of St. Petersburg's royalty and aristocracy, are now being restored by a Western-backed foundation. But disputed investment laws, historic preservationists, and traditional Russian xenophobia have made European-funded preservation projects controversial, including the renovation of the tsarist-era Hotel Astoria (facing page).*

One of the more controversial redevelopment projects is the deal for New Holland, a run-down collection of red-brick workshops and warehouses used by the Russian navy. A French company, a division of Compagnie General des Eaux, created a joint venture with Russian developers to turn New Holland —a naval warehouse since the eighteenth century— into a $500-million complex complete with artists' studios, dockside cafés, and a pedestrian mall lined with luxury shops. Backed by the mayor and city planners, the joint venture won a ninety-nine-year lease on New Holland. But the low-priced lease and the ambitious French architectural plans sparked the city council to accuse the mayor of selling out to "foreign land grabbers." In response, the price of the lease was increased, and the French agreed to let the Russian developers control the restoration of the facade. The French will share interior restoration with other investors.

City council was not the only protester. The island's residents, the Russian navy, at first tried to torpedo the project, complaining that the facilities there—including a deep tank where scale models of new warships were tested—were irreplaceable. The New Holland developers, however, have begun building suitable facilities elsewhere in St. Petersburg to which the navy is slowly relocating. "Now it is just a question of waiting," says New Holland's optimistic general director, Grigory Galibov, though he concedes it will be 1996 before the unwanted tenants can relocate completely and real development on New Holland can begin.

The first public controversy over development in the city's historic center was an angry confrontation in 1987 and 1988 over the restoration of two landmark imperial-era hotels. The uproar pitted a coalition of environmentalists and preservationists, many of them students, against Communist Party bosses who were forced to defend their decisions in a hostile court of public opinion. Today the ruckus created by the demolition of the Angleterre and the rehabilitation of the adjacent Astoria is remembered as a watershed in local politics. For history buffs, the uproar helped save a landmark—the Astoria—where American journalist John Reed watched the 1917 October Revo-

lution from the bar before writing *Ten Days That Shook the World*.

A Finnish wrecking crew made short work of the old Angleterre, which, after being completely rebuilt, is now an upscale address for international visitors. But placard-carrying preservationists, aided by an increasingly unfettered press, succeeded in igniting a fiery debate over how to preserve the city's rich architectural heritage from an onslaught of modern architecture. Aroused by forty years of Soviet-style building that can only be described as "heartless functionalism," activists in the 1980s campaigned to halt development that already had turned St. Petersburg's suburbs into an anonymous tumble of apartment buildings and factories that look old before their time.

"Historic preservation and environmentalism were the only legitimate vehicles to express anti-Communism," says Blair Ruble, director of the Kennan Center for Advanced Russian Studies in Washington, D.C., who watched the confrontation firsthand. "This was the flash point out of which came organizations and informal networks for the new politics that challenged Communist control." The affaire Angleterre ushered in a new city council made up of liberal reformers and anti-Communist "democrats." But with the collapse of Communism in 1991, the unity of these activists has shattered, and there still is no coherent plan to preserve historic St. Petersburg.

"This city is blessed with more cultural real estate than any other city in Russia," says Valentin Nazarov, director of the city's Masterplan Institute, which is charged with devising a new master plan that will take the city into the next century. "We cannot continue to throw these buildings in the garbage dump because the military-industrial complex wants its way. The Cold War is over."

But for all of the grand plans, only a handful of multinational firms have so far received leases to historic buildings, given them a facelift, and opened up for business. Chief among these are the Swedish hotel group Reso, which refurbished the elegant Grand Hotel Europa, and the French banking giant Crédit Lyonnais.

The city, meanwhile, uses revenues from these leases and money from historic buildings leased to a handful of Russian-owned businesses to continue long-standing projects like the restoration of Catherine and Gatchina palaces and the renovation of the Church of the Resurrection just off Nevsky Prospekt along Griboyedov Canal on the spot where Tsar Aleksandr II was assassinated in 1881. The fanciful mosaics with gilded onion domes complete a twenty-year-long restoration. But beyond evicting a few military schools and discredited Communist bureaucrats from landmark icons like the Stroganov and blood-red Beloselsky-Belozersky palaces, little else seems to have changed since the Communists ruled the city from elegant quarters in the Mariinsky Palace and Smolny Institute.

UNESCO's theoretical protection of the downtown and suburban palaces has thwarted encroachment from skyscrapers and unwelcome renters. At UNESCO's Paris headquarters, officials note that the organization is chartered to provide technical assistance, not to bankroll the massive restoration of St. Petersburg envisioned by some city planners and international developers. Ultimately, says one UNESCO official, the city will have to take responsibility for its future and devise a comprehensive plan to protect the buildings of its noble past.

PASSAZH,
*a glass-covered art
nouveau depart-
ment store on
Nevsky Prospekt,
has undergone a
facelift, returning
the two-story
arcade to its late
nineteenth-century
glory with an
array of small
shops that sell
everything from
housewares to
liquor (facing page,
c. 1910). City plan-
ners are pushing
an ambitious
scheme to build St.
Petersburg's first
Western-style shop-
ping mall just off
Nevsky Prospekt—
if they can obtain
the financing and
leases to the build-
ings. The $200-mil-
lion dream project
would include
artists' studios,
boutiques, theaters,
office space, and
a hotel in* Apraksin
Dvor, *now a
backwater where
flea marketers
rendezvous.*

"Then long we suffered in retreat,
All keen the enemy to meet..."

MIKHAIL LERMONTOV
BORODINO, 1837

BREAKING THE ECONOMIC ICE

Every morning at eight o'clock sharp, a ceremonial bugle call from the cruiser *Aurora* punctuates the early bustle along the Neva, and sailors raise a blue-and-white flag first hoisted by the founder of the imperial navy, Peter the Great. Gone are the colors of the old Soviet navy, the red hammer-and-sickle that flew over the *Aurora* and ships of the line for more than seven decades of Communism. The flag replacing it—a blue St. Andrew's cross on a white field—symbolizes Russia's access to four great seas during Peter's reign and has its roots in more than a thousand years of Byzantine history.

When the Russian government ordered Peter's flag hoisted at Navy Day ceremonies in 1992, thousands lined the Petrograd embankment of the Neva. Thousands more watched from small boats or on television, so great was St. Petersburg's pride in the navy and its founder. A long line of modern warships rode at anchor in the Neva channel, their guns and missile tubes aimed skyward beneath a constellation of semaphore flags. Sailors shouted three hurrahs in unison for passing admirals.

Tied to four giant moorings, the *Aurora* appeared to sag under the weight of priests of the Russian Orthodox Church, military and city officials, naval attachés resplendent in gold braid, war veterans, journalists and photographers from around the world. Priests sprinkled holy water on the new flag and blessed it three times as is the tradition of the Russian Orthodox Church. And in a stunning gesture that reflected the changes sweeping Russia, admirals and clergymen embraced in hearty bear hugs and gentle kisses on the gangway beneath the *Aurora*'s three smokestacks. Vice Admiral Igor Kudryashov, chief of staff of the St. Petersburg naval district, read the general orders

THE VENERABLE WARSHIP

Aurora *(facing page), from which the shot was fired that signaled the storming of the Winter Palace in 1917, was refurbished in the 1980s and remains in active service as a naval cadet training vessel and military museum.*

CHAPTER THREE

OLD RUSSIAN TRADITIONS *are being revived
at Kronstadt, where Orthodox priests (above) bless the restoration of a
naval ensign that was designed by Peter the Great. Warships of the Baltic
Fleet (facing page) ride at anchor in the Neva for Navy Day ceremonies.*

restoring the flag of St. Andrew's cross. He recounted how Peter ordered construction of Russia's first seagoing vessels in 1696—the year officially designated as the birth of the Russian navy. A flag followed soon afterward, its X-shaped cross honoring the martyred saint who, according to Russian folklore, first preached Christianity to the eastern Slavs.

Amid all the clamor, much of the city's pride inevitably focused on the *Aurora*, a ship that has called St. Petersburg home since joining the Baltic Fleet in 1903. Many in the crowd saw irony in the government's decision to raise the flag of tsarist Russia from the steel gray fantail of the old *Aurora*. History had come full circle for a city and a ship whose destinies were joined. For the history of the *Aurora* is almost as illustrious as the flag it flies. During the disastrous Russo-Japanese War of 1904–5, the *Aurora* steamed from nearby Kronstadt Naval Base more than halfway around the world—18,305 miles in 224 days—into

harm's way at the battle of Tsushima Strait off the Korean peninsula. She took eighteen direct hits from Japanese warships in a ruinous four-hour engagement that decimated the Russian fleet. But the *Aurora* was repaired and saw more action in October 1917, when her six-inch forecastle gun fired the shot that signaled the storming of the Winter Palace, just downriver from the cruiser's present-day moorings. The shot—a blank —brought the Bolsheviks to power and assured the *Aurora* a place in Communist mythology. More than two decades later, during the bitter siege of Leningrad, its heavy guns were dismounted and moved inland for firepower in a pitched tank battle with Nazis in 1941. Refurbished in the 1980s at St. Petersburg's Severnaya Wharf shipyard, the awkward gray lady became a training ship for cadets and midshipmen at nearby schools, as well as a naval museum.

Though the Russian navy has regained its colors, it sails rough seas beyond St. Petersburg. Political and

economic storms have taken much of the glamour and prestige out of navy service today. And officers are far from calm. "For generations," says Admiral Kudryashov, a robust, square-jawed sailor with two decades of service in the Northern Fleet before coming to St. Petersburg, "the navy was considered the 'white bone' [blue blood] of the Russian military. But no more. These are difficult times for patriots."

The end of the Cold War now draws fewer officers and sailors to St. Petersburg's five naval academies, including the Frunze Naval War College where future admirals are minted. Some ten shipyards and repair facilities on the Neva and its tributaries turn out fewer warships and submarines. Even Kronstadt, a key Baltic Fleet training and supply base seventeen miles from St. Petersburg on Kotlin Island, is not immune from the changes. Strapped for cash for fuel and sailors' salaries, Russia's once-mighty Baltic squadrons from St. Petersburg are staying closer to home. At the height of the Cold War, cruisers and destroyers out of Kronstadt roamed the oceans from Cuba to Vietnam, but no more. Now, only Russia's ballistic-missile-firing nuclear submarines patrol far from home waters. And Kronstadt, with five huge dry docks, is being eyed as a new "free-enterprise zone" akin to Hong Kong or Dubai. Officials in the mayor's office talk of turning some of the old fortresses into hotels or

casinos and of opening a yacht club to attract visitors. Meanwhile, navy officers with years of service are being mustered out to face an uncertain future after crash courses in market economics and résumé writing.

Even the new flag has yet to win acceptance. "Changing the flag is humiliating for many of us," says Commander Aleksandr Danchenko, a staff officer at St. Petersburg headquarters. "Our greatest victories were won under the red banner [of the Soviet navy], and now we are asked to return to this St. Andrew's flag by politicians who never served a day in uniform." His bitterness is shared by Andrei Sergeyev, a submariner. "To tell you the truth," he says, "it makes my soul hurt because I know my grandfathers spilled their blood for both flags."

On a dark back street, near where the Admiralty Canal intersects the Moika, lies a nervous giant—a bunker-like fortress called the Admiralty Shipyard. It is one of ten yards and repair facilities that made St. Petersburg one of the largest naval bases in all of the now-shattered Soviet Union. But unlike other St. Petersburg defense plants that are eager to attract investors from abroad, the Admiralty remains restricted to international journalists. *Glasnost*, or openness, has its limits, correspondents are told, even

SAILORS LET OFF STEAM

in Palace Square (above), while cadets at St. Petersburg's Nakhimov
Naval School (facing page) study Russian literature in addition to
seamanship. As former Soviet bases are closed in Germany and the
Baltic states, scores of ships and submarines are being shifted to nearby
Kronstadt, an island citadel, with fifty-five thousand residents, built
by Peter the Great on the site of a Swedish garrison.

though the superpower rivalry is officially over.

An innocent-looking time and temperature sign at the shipyard gate belies darker activities inside. Here cruise-missile-firing Victor III–class submarines, 351-foot (107-meter) behemoths of the deep that guarantee Russia's continued status as a nuclear power, are crafted inside a concrete hangar-like pen that remains impervious to spy satellites. The pen's doors open onto the Neva only at night. When a Victor III slips into the Neva—an occasion never announced—it is powered by twin atomic reactors that turn some of the quietest, stealthiest propellers in the world of naval engineering.

The first Admiralty Shipyard was founded by Peter in November 1704 on the south bank of the Neva opposite the Peter and Paul Fortress. Now St. Petersburg's most prominent landmark with its 238-foot (72.5-meter) gilded spire, the Admiralty became the city's first factory and the birthplace of Russia's first battleship, the fifty-four-cannon *Poltava*. Today the Admiralty is the local headquarters of the Russian navy.

Shipbuilding passed in 1856 to Baltiisky Zavod on Vasilyevsky Island near where the Neva makes a jagged turn toward the Gulf of Finland. Over the next 150 years, the Baltic Shipyard would become a leading manufacturer of surface warships, including four nuclear-powered dreadnoughts of the Kirov class—the Russian navy's largest and newest guided-missile cruisers. But of all other St. Petersburg yards, which make everything from nuclear-powered submarines to hydrofoil hovercraft for amphibious assaults by Russian marines, Baltiisky has taken the lead in throwing open its doors to visitors and businesses from the West.

Oleg Shulyekovsky, the shipyard's dynamic general manager, is doing more than just talking about *konversiya*—or conversion—the painful disarmament process that has become a post–Cold War buzzword. He already has turned the Baltic yard into a private company owned by employees and outside stockholders. And he has attracted customers in countries that used to be called the enemy. "It's hard to say where we are headed after the Cold War," confesses Shulyekovsky, a naval engineer by training. "But our enterprise has captured the attention of German and American businesses with the quality of our work and cheap labor." For a yard that relied on the navy of the collapsed Soviet Union for 80 percent of its orders as recently as 1989, the shipyard now has scaled back military production to about 7 percent.

The Baltic Shipyard's last big-ticket navy order, the *Peter the Great*, has been tied up on the Neva for years, a relic of the Cold War before it sets sail. More like a battleship than fast cruiser, the *Pyotr Veliky* was designed to protect Soviet aircraft carriers, but those carriers already have been mothballed to save money or have been scrapped. *Pyotr* is destined to join the Pacific Fleet at Vladivostok, but a political fight over who owns the nuclear muscle of the old Soviet navy forced the Baltiisky to stretch out completion of the warship. Its two nuclear reactors are something of a Baltic Shipyard specialty, says Shulyekovsky. Besides producing heavy cruisers, Baltiisky has twenty-five years of experience making mammoth atomic-powered icebreakers, which are named after cities and regions in Siberia.

"We have the credentials to make civilian atomic-powered ships," says chief engineer Yevgeny Shanin. "We wrote the book." But in an era when the word "atomic" evokes images of Chernobyl, not Acapulco, no cruise ship company has come forward with a scheme to lure tourists aboard a nuclear-powered liner. Orders for any kind of passenger ships have not materialized, in part because Western partners prefer to outfit their own ships with state-of-the-art navigational and electronic systems and world-class luxury. In the meantime, Baltiisky has kept a scaled-down workforce busy making low-cost chemical carriers and so-called roll-on roll-off cargo ships.

By the end of the Cold War, four industries drove the economy of what was then Leningrad: ship- and machine-building, precision instruments, and electronics. To speed production, assembly lines at some five hundred factories were linked by an incestuous web of financial and Communist Party ties to 150 scientific research and design centers. One-quarter of all Leningraders were involved in scientific work, making it the second most important technical center in the Soviet Union after Moscow.

But it was applied science with a perverse twist. Fully 80 percent of the city's 230,000 scientists and technicians worked in military plants or on military-related research, according to Russian and Western intelligence assessments. Even more startling, 75 percent of the city's industrial production went to the military—the army, navy, air force, strategic nuclear forces, and the KGB border guards. Thousands of uniformed officers were assigned to factories and laboratories, giving Leningrad the feeling of a garrison on a constant state of alert.

"Leningrad was like the whole state of California during the Cold War," says Dr. Daniel Aleksandrov, a researcher at the Institute of the History of Science and Technology in St. Petersburg. "It was the center of

THIS ENSIGN *of St. Andrew's Cross and three stars (above) signifies the presence on board this ship of a vice admiral of the Russian navy. Recruits at Kronstadt Naval Base (facing page) are all smiles for visitors to the restricted fortress.*

military R&D [research and development]." Many of the city's fifty-two institutions of higher learning, including an array of vocational and technical schools, churned out a steady stream of graduates for about three hundred R&D institutes and laboratories with military ties.

"The system was unique to Leningrad," says Aleksandrov, scion of a prominent scientific family. "But what have they got to show for all this R&D? Most of the new exciting stuff came from abroad, even in high-energy physics and the A-bomb. Now science in Petersburg is like a whale on the beach dying of its own weight. It got too big."

With the Cold War now so much history, St. Petersburg is burdened with a scientific elite and outdated defense industries that are virtually broke. Scientists are going abroad in droves or going to work for multinational companies or other governments eager to keep them out of the employ of militant states such as Libya or North Korea. And some defense factory managers, emboldened by a conservative backlash opposed to Moscow's economic reforms, want to continue making arms to sell to the highest bidder in places like the Middle East and Asia. Meanwhile, politicians who have embraced the West, capitalism, and the high-tech consumer age keep talking about *konversiya*. They want to retool the decaying industrial belts that ring St. Petersburg's suburbs and line the Neva. Local politicians and their legion of Western advisers think defense factories can meet the pent-up

GANTRY CRANES *in the main channel of the Neva (left) dwarf the Kirov-class guided-missile cruiser* Peter the Great, *the last nuclear-powered dreadnought built by the Baltic Shipyard. Welders and engineers who install atomic reactors receive extra food in the yard's cafeteria (above).*

demands of Russian consumers and attract non-Russian customers with highly skilled cheap labor.

Sober assessments are, however, almost as common as sailors on Nevsky Prospekt. One Western economist compares the daunting task to an entire city learning to drive on the right-hand side of the road after generations of driving on the left—multiplied a hundredfold by the complexity of the changeover from war to something approaching peace. "This is the ultimate cold shower for St. Petersburg," says a Western intelligence analyst with firsthand experience in the old tsarist capital.

But Professor Zhores Alferov, chairman of the Russian Academy of Sciences' Scientific Center and a nuclear physicist at the Ioffe Physical-Technical Institute, is more optimistic. "Only 10 percent, not 90 percent, of St. Petersburg needs conversion," he contends. "Our basic industries like electronics are strong. This is the center of microprocessors, radio electronics like TVs and VCRs, and all kinds of optics. It's only the specialized research institutes that are badly affected."

Konversiya is gathering momentum as defense giants find Western partners with money and technology to invest. The Arsenal Factory now makes refrigerators and air compressors alongside 110mm naval guns and platforms for spy satellites. And the huge Bolshevik plant, maker of railroad cars for Russia's rail-mobile SS-24 intercontinental nuclear missile force, is trying its hand at wheelchairs, oil drilling equipment, steam irons, and other household appliances.

Other military titans are setting their sights on Western capital. With fifty thousand employees, the Leninets Association makes aircraft radars and aircraft computers in sixteen factories, ten research institutes, and fifty smaller workshops. Leninets also has taken the lead in organizing the Engineering Center for Conversion and has retooled some assembly lines to make diagnostic and rehabilitative medical equipment. With the help of an $80 million investment from the Gillette Company of the United States, Leninets is building a factory to make shaving products, which are nearly as precious as gold bullion in proletarian Russia.

Meanwhile, recruiters from Western universities and research centers scramble to hire some of Russia's ablest scientific talent. Already 60 percent of the faculty at the Petersburg Institute of Mathematics and 15

GRIPPED IN WINTER'S *sub-zero embrace, St. Petersburg's port (facing page)—now Russia's busiest—groans under strains brought on by the collapse of the Soviet Union. With Baltic and Black Sea harbors controlled by restive new governments, millions of extra tons of cargo are squeezed through St. Petersburg. A flotilla of icebreakers keeps the channel open year round, though nuclear-powered icebreakers, like this one (above) under construction at the Baltic Shipyard, are used only in the Arctic.*

"THAT'S NOT ICE," *scoffs Vadim Shuvalov, assistant general manager of the St. Petersburg Commercial Seaport, where a fleet of icebreakers keeps the channel open. "We call it ice when it's a meter [3.3 feet] deep." Situated just below the Arctic Circle at 59°55′N, the overburdened port handles more than a million tons a month. But the line of ships is sometimes so drawn-out that port authorities say, only half in jest, that it may be the longest queue in Russia.*

percent of the physicists at the Ioffe Physical-Technical Institute have gone abroad on "contracts," the euphemism favored to describe a brain drain to the West. Others have chosen to stay in St. Petersburg to work on research projects financed by Western companies. New York–based Corning Incorporated has hired 115 scientists and technicians at the Vavilov State Optical Institute, maker of cameras for spy satellites and lasers for a Soviet "star wars" space-based missile defense system, and the Institute for Silicate Chemistry, which specializes in the study of useful forms of glass. At European trade shows, Vavilov's advertising features such exotic products as multipath interferometers; marine navigational signals, beacons, and lighthouses; zinc selenide for lasers; space and laser optics; glass-crystalline mirrors; and infrared imagers.

Armed with cellular telephones, international executives and their Russian partners prowl St. Petersburg for high-tech bargains. Cheap integrated circuits, specialized magnets, and laser optics are high on their lists. Says an American business consultant in a posh hotel bar: "Some of the Russian microelectronics are as good as we have in the West; some are better; and some you can't find anywhere else in the world."

Even with outside investment, many plants will be

BLAST FURNACES *at the Kirov Metalworks (right) forge hundreds of tons of high-grade steel each day. But commercial tractors (below) have replaced T-80 main battle tanks on Kirov assembly lines. The breakup of St. Petersburg defense plants, brought on by the sharp drop in armaments orders, has raised fears of widespread unemployment.*

split up, shrunk, or closed, including the giant Kirov Metalworks, where T-80 tanks, the heavy punch of the much-feared Soviet blitzkrieg across Western Europe, were designed and built until 1992. So far Kirov's attempt to step up production of a new line of tractors on the former tank assembly line has failed to quell the fear of large-scale unemployment—something unknown during the days of Soviet Communism when everyone was guaranteed a job. But says one Western defense analyst: "Petersburg is luckier than some cities. It was never a one-horse town, making only tanks or submarines. Its scientists designed the war machine, but there was always a civilian economy. Petersburg has

the potential to turn the high-tech sector into something really useful." St. Petersburg is betting its future on it.

The offerings on the "big board" at the St. Petersburg Commodities and Stock Exchange confirm that the city remains Russia's "window to the West" of Pushkin's poem. The *birzha,* as the exchange is called—echoing the word "bourse" long-favored by Europeans —is the province of young Russians schooled in the ways of capitalism. Moving fast this morning are red salmon from the Pacific coast port of Vladivostok,

ALWAYS RUSSIA'S WINDOW *to the West,*
St. Petersburg garners trade shows and international commerce.
A red Ferrari dazzles the curious at an automobile exhibition (above),
while brokers at the St. Petersburg Commodities and Stock
Exchange (facing page) haggle over everything from salmon to stock
certificates in formerly state-owned factories.

orange juice from Germany, American canned beer, and rice from Thailand. The array of goods for sale is dizzying: Japanese panty hose, English shirts, Russian cars, American butter, Korean running shoes, Polish vodka, gasoline, honey, milk, construction materials, and potato peelers.

All goods are bought in Russian rubles, though American dollars can be changed into rubles by bank affiliates in the exchange. Almost everything will end up in new private shops along Nevsky Prospekt and main streets or kiosks, where Western economists see a grassroots market economy taking shape. Another promising sign: alongside foodstuffs, companies are bartering stock certificates. Some stock offerings in this brave new world of capitalism are for state-run defense plants, which are trying to meet a government deadline to reorganize as private firms along several Western models. Already more state-owned businesses have been turned over to private investors in St. Petersburg than in any other city in Russia.

The bourse acts like an intermediary, providing a wholesale market in a country that has run on centralized state planning dictated from Moscow for more than sixty years. Like commodities exchanges in the West, it has even begun dealing in futures. Director of a nearby securities exchange, Igor Klyuchnikov thinks the St. Petersburg bourse is "more like a little bazaar now, not like an American-style stock exchange." Just the same, he says, a new breed of Russian capitalists is "creating opportunities as the old communist system is disintegrating."

"I get very frustrated and depressed by these young businessmen who buy up everything for their private kiosks and private restaurants," says Yekaterina Boitseva, a twenty-six-year-old broker, tossing her red hair in the direction of the big board. "Sometimes there is nothing left for ordinary people like myself." On most mornings, Boitseva watches food offerings for state-run grocery stores. One of more than two hundred fifty licensed brokers, Boitseva must decide what's *goryacheye*—hot—and what her clients can afford amid the mass confusion of the trading floors.

St. Petersburg's exchange floor is frugal. There are a few Western style *kompyutery*, including several *leptops*, wired into an illuminated scoreboard suspended over the main hall and also a bell to open and close trading. There are display cases for imported and locally made goods on the market, and a TV monitor

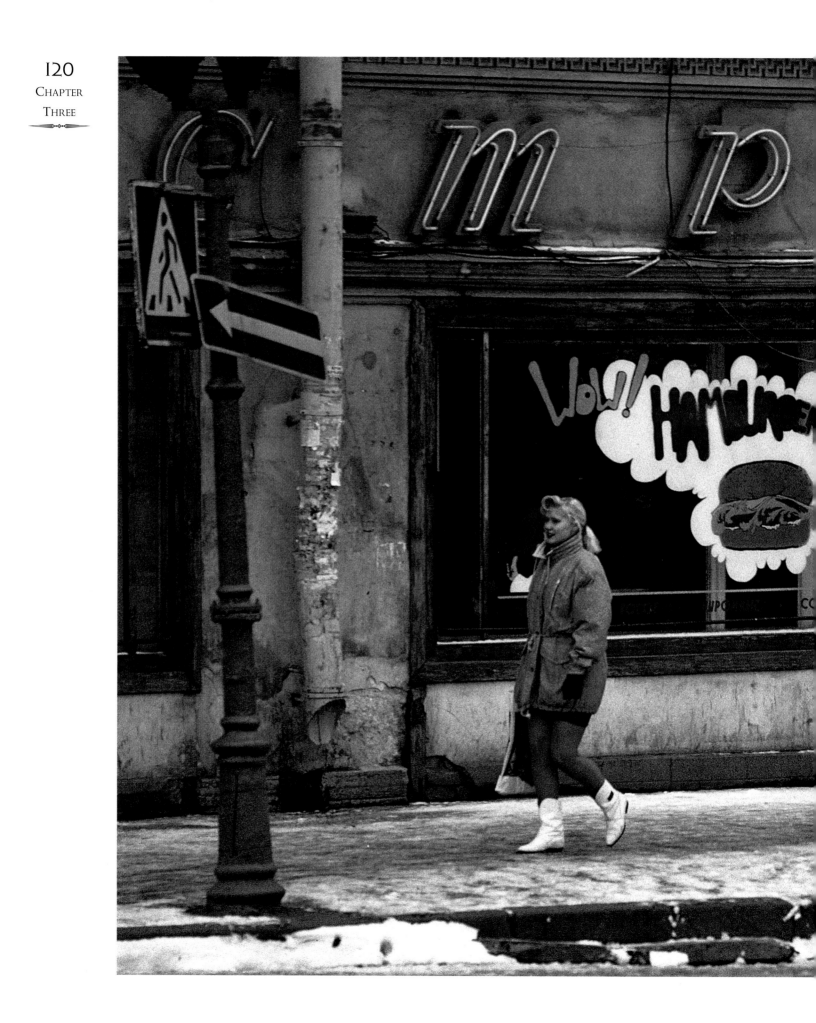

ENGLISH
IS THE
*language of many
enterprising
Petersburgers, who
have formed part-
nerships with
scores of interna-
tional companies—
or struck out on
their own in street-
corner kiosks and
Western-style
restaurants. As
Russia's second
largest city, St.
Petersburg has its
share of self-made
millionaires, but
many merchants
say they are
threatened by
extortionists
demanding
"protection"
money.*

I C E C R E A M S A L E S *are brisk, even in the dead of winter (above). But officials worry that young people are increasingly attracted to easy street-side commerce (right), shunning studies in the arts and sciences at St. Petersburg's more than fifty institutions of higher learning.*

tuned to CNN International—another measure of status among newly rich Russians. The parking lot of the St. Petersburg bourse is filled with *Bemvushkas,* BMW sedans from Germany much coveted by Russian yuppies on the way up.

Peter the Great founded the first exchange in 1709. By the time Lenin and his Bolsheviks came to power in 1917, there were eight exchanges. Now St. Petersburg boasts five that have weathered the survival of the fittest after an initial explosion of some twenty exchanges in the city. And while the exchanges don't look like the Chicago Board of Trade or Wall Street yet, they are driven by the same reasons that spur pandemonium in the West. Industries and entrepreneurs have goods to sell or barter. To no one's surprise, Western economists say that what drives brokers—and the Russian market—is the expectation of making money.

Everyone in St. Petersburg seems to have heard a story about someone becoming a millionaire overnight, and they want to join the action. St. Petersburg is estimated to have at least 200,000 newly rich citizens with monthly incomes approaching $1,000—enough to allow them to enjoy a comfortable standard of living on a par with Western Europe or America.

International economists and Russian government officials, however, worry that many exchanges are

THE NEED TO EARN *extra rubles does not escape the elderly for whom Russia has little social security. On Nevsky Prospekt, St. Petersburg's main street, a woman (facing page) hawks a doll to tourists. Babushki—a Russian term of affection for women past a certain age— sell flowers (below) in front of the Kuznechny Market, though many say they are humiliated by the need to supplement their state-paid pensions.*

unregulated and subject to "insider trading" by corrupt administrators of state-owned businesses. Instead of selling directly to customers, some businesses sell products—crude oil, timber, strategic metals—at artificially low rates to commodities brokers, who then jack up the price and share profits with the "insider" at the state-owned company. Local businessmen also complain of having to pay enormous bribes, often to corrupt government officials, to open stores or get export licenses in the lucrative trade in raw materials from Russia's rich hinterlands. And rival gangs, often called "mafias," extort millions in protection money, leading some in business to form their own private armies of bodyguards.

Meanwhile, St. Petersburg police and Russian customs officers say unscrupulous defense plant workers have teamed up with smugglers to export illegally thousands of tons of high-grade nickel, aluminum, and

bronze to the West. The mountains of metal disappearing from St. Petersburg arms factories is partially responsible for a dramatic one-third decline in the world price of nickel in 1992, according to authorities in Russia and the London Metals Exchange. Smugglers run convoys along secret routes cut through forests southwest of St. Petersburg to the Baltic states and eventually Western Europe, generating billions of dollars in illegal profits along the way. In 1993, for example, a ton of nickel bought at a St. Petersburg defense factory for $2,500 commanded $4,700 in Latvia, where intermediaries turned around and sold it for about $6,000 a ton.

The unsettling economic and social changes sweeping Russia are felt just as keenly on the Strelka, a spit of land opposite the Winter Palace where the Neva divides, and the adjacent byways of Vasilyevsky Island. On a wide semicircular campus of colonnaded neoclassical buildings painted pale yellow and red, Russian science is fighting for its life. This is where Lomonosov first looked at the heavens from the Kunstkammer and wrote about chemistry in

Latin. St. Petersburg State University, second largest in Russia, occupies the building of the Twelve Colleges —the first government office commissioned by Peter the Great. The chemist Dmitry Mendeleyev devised his periodic table of elements in a university laboratory. Here, too, are lodged the independent institutes of zoology, ethnology, geology, psychology, molecular biology, and Russian literature, plus the Academy of Sciences, with its Scientific Center and cavernous library. And next door to a student cafeteria sits the once supersecret Vavilov State Optical Institute, the world's biggest optical research center and maker of spy satellite cameras. Military officers in gray wool greatcoats mingle with students in blue jeans and gaily colored down parkas.

Science historian Daniel Aleksandrov calls the Strelka campus the "core of old Russian science." This is where theoretical research—what Aleksandrov calls "high science"—was always more prized than lucrative R&D contracts for the ubiquitous Red Army. "Thank God," says Aleksandrov, "there are people who still want to collect butterflies instead of go into business for themselves." But that number, never large, may be shrinking.

HALLS OF ACADEMIA *stretch through the cavernous 1,300-foot-long (400-meter-long) Collegia or main building of St. Petersburg State University, where a student crams for an examination (facing page). In the university cafeteria (above), students voice their frustration with old-fashioned courses and out-of-date facilities. Second largest in Russia, the university opened in 1819.*

SCHOLARS FILL ONE
*of the reading rooms (right) of the National Library
of Russia, formerly the Saltykov-Shchedrin. Equivalent
of the U.S. Library of Congress, the library counts
twenty-two million books and periodicals in its collection, including manuscripts in Peter the Great's own
hand. International exchange students (below) frequent the library, but few new books, magazines, or
newspapers from abroad have been purchased since
Russia slipped into an economic crisis.*

DMITRY MENDELEYEV,
*one of St. Petersburg's scientific elite, devised
the periodic table of elements (below), which is
emblazoned on the side of a technical school on
Moscow Prospekt. At the Vavilov Plant Industry
Institute (facing page), seeds of plants, such as
drought-resistant wheat, barley, and corn, were
gathered by Nikolai Vavilov in Africa earlier in
this century. Later the plants vanished from Africa
for several years, and now these seeds in the
Vavilov collection have been returned to the famine-
ridden land to revive its agriculture. About $1.5
million in international aid has been proposed to
preserve the facility's collection, which is the
second largest seed bank in the world and includes
seeds of thousands of now-extinct plants.*

Many students who once planned scientific careers say they are putting their dreams on hold, dropping out of school to earn quick cash in new businesses or street-corner speculation. They are part of a colossal "internal brain drain" that alarms administrators such as the Academy of Sciences' Alferov, who doubles as chairman of its St. Petersburg Scientific Center. "Forget the scientists who have gone abroad," booms Alferov, a nuclear physicist well known in international circles. "These scientists are gone, though we hope some will come back." Far more alarming for the future, he says, is the "internal leakage of our brightest minds" into oftentimes shady business deals euphemistically called "commercial structures."

"They're lost!" booms Alferov. "It will be impossible to retrain them. We must prepare a new generation."

But instilling a Western-style work ethic in a new generation of St. Petersburg students is easier said than done. Petersburgers, like their compatriots, are products of a great Russian culture that respects power, including the power of money, in a world suddenly turned upside down.

Listening to vintage Elvis Presley music on a jukebox in the university cafeteria, Boris Schor, a third-year genetics student, settles down for a quick lunch —fish sandwich and red beet salad washed down with lukewarm coffee. "I'm not necessarily pessimistic about finding a job," says Schor, who supplements his trivial student stipend by translating American scientific journals. "But I know how far behind we are. Students have no PCs, no chance to read the latest scientific literature, no money. There is very little motivation to learn," he says.

Meanwhile, some research institutes hope to stay alive with Western aid. "Without international contacts," says the Russian Academy's Alferov, "science in St. Petersburg will not survive."

Nowhere is this better illustrated than at the Vavilov Plant Industry Institute (known by its Russian acronym VIR), the world's second largest seed bank and repository of 380,000 strains of plant and food crops at last count. A $1.5 million rescue plan has been proposed by the United States Department of Agriculture, and with the initial funds from this plan, VIR's scientists are cataloging the collection into an international data base using American PCs. Because

so much Russian scientific endeavor was closed for so long, opening up the Vavilov collection and making sense of it is nearly as electrifying as opening King Tutankhamen's tomb, says an American scientist. "Except in this case," suggests Doctor Henry Shands of USDA, "everything is alive. We're excited."

No relation to the Vavilov Institute that makes spy satellite cameras, this institute on St. Isaac's Square is named for Nikolai Vavilov, a plant collector and geographer who trekked across five continents during the 1920s and 1930s, gathering cultivated plants and their wild relatives. Vavilov wanted to help people grow more wheat, corn, rice, and potatoes. Using the then-new science of genetics, he bred one plant with another to make them resist disease or drought or adapt to a different region. Before he died in prison under Stalin, Vavilov amassed the first seed bank ever created.

Far ahead of his time, Vavilov devised a revolutionary theory about the origins of most of the world's food plants. Though his theory has been modified over the years, it has gained wide acceptance. Vavilov postulated that virtually all of the world's food crops and feed grains come from about 130 plant species, most first cultivated in the Stone Age. These plants have their roots in a dozen or more ancestral homes near the high mountain ranges of the Himalayan, Hindu Kush, and Andes, and lesser mountains of the Middle East, Balkans, and Apennines.

Today, Vavilov's seed collection remains in bins and paper bags in the old imperial Ministry of Agriculture buildings in downtown St. Petersburg, as well as in cold storage in southern Russia at the Kuban Experimental Station near Krasnodar. Western scientists say this is some of the most valuable genetic

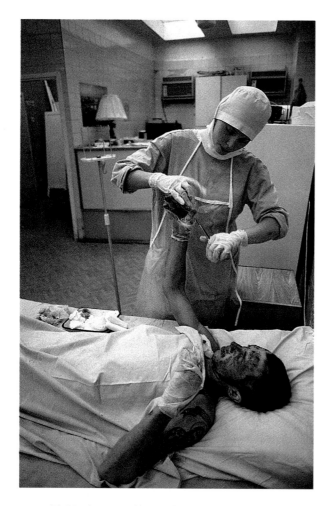

THE MEDICAL STAFF

*at Djanelidze Emergency Medicine Institute treats
some twenty-three thousand patients each year, often
comparing their work to service in a combat zone.
Nurse Irina Gun (above) changes the dressings of a
burn victim, and a quiet moment is found in the
hospital cafeteria (facing page).*

material in the world, including twenty-five thousand
samples of rare wild plants that could one day save a
country or a continent from famine. The institute owns
the largest collection of potato seeds on the planet—
some twenty-five hundred strains, including wild
potatoes Vavilov collected sixty years ago in Peru—at
a rundown experimental station in suburban Pavlovsk
about a forty-five-minute drive from downtown St.
Petersburg. So primitive are the VIR storage facilities
that more than a thousand strains of plants are replant-
ed each year and their offspring harvested for fresh
genetic stock. Otherwise the seeds would rot. Vegetable
seeds that would last two hundred years in heat-sealed
foil pouches in Western laboratories spoil in five years
in the dampness and mildew of St. Petersburg.

In addition to the USDA, the international rescue
effort of VIR may be backed by the World Bank, the
Rockefeller Foundation, and the United Nations
Development Program. For Doctor Viktor Dragavtsev,
the institute's director, the proposed international aid
effort offers hope. "The fate of the collection is, at best,
uncertain," he says, pacing back and forth in front of a
map of Vavilov's countless expeditions. "This institute
is a resource for the whole world, but first we must
keep it alive."

After seed banks were plundered in war- and
drought-ravaged Ethiopia and Somalia, African agronomists and the International Board for Plant Genetic
Resources turned to VIR for help—an ironic last-ditch
plea, considering the economic collapse of Russia.
Dragavtsev and his colleagues searched VIR's endless
dark rooms in St. Petersburg, finally discovering seeds
collected in Africa decades ago by Nikolai Vavilov
himself—drought-resistant wheat, barley, sorghum,
corn, and beans, more than fifty species in all. Too
poor to afford high-priced international couriers, VIR
scientists simply dropped the seeds in the mail in plain
paper envelopes, hoping to jump-start agriculture on
the embattled Horn of Africa. Dragavetsev calls VIR's
gesture modest. But African agronomists call the seeds
priceless gifts from a city that prizes science and learning—gifts that will help rebuild agriculture in a region
grown accustomed to international food handouts in
the best of times.

Another international aid effort is saving more than
seeds in St. Petersburg. It is saving lives. Surgeons

and nurses in the burn unit of Djanelidze Emergency Medicine Institute race the clock to save two critically injured women with third-degree burns over 75 percent of their bodies. High-intensity surgical lamps guide the quick hands of Doctor Dmitry Pryutu, who cuts away huge swathes of black, charred skin. Nurse Irina Gun covers the wounds with a white ointment called Silvadene cream as if she were caressing the *Mona Lisa*. The burn victims—one set afire in an industrial accident, the other in a family quarrel—are wrapped head to toe in gauze. The two operations take less than fifteen minutes.

Later, as doctors and nurses unwind in a staff lounge at Russia's premier trauma center in a St. Petersburg suburb, they consider the "wonder ointment"—an antibiotic called silver sulfadiazene—that fights infection. A giant U.S. Air Force C-5A Galaxy cargo jet delivered the medication in 1992 to St. Petersburg from American war stocks still in Europe—stockpiles that have been turned into depots of humanitarian aid since the breakup of the Soviet Union. The ointment comes in a large blue container that bears the ubiquitous sign of Washington bureaucracy, a Federal stock number.

"We have some rough equivalents," explains Doctor Mikhail Krylov, chief of the burn unit. "But our drugs are practically never available. Only Silvadene saves lives quite like this." Showing off the antibiotic cream as if it were a treasure in a St. Petersburg museum, Krylov says in a voice resonating with emotion: "This is from the war we didn't fight. It's yours, it's American."

"Here is courage. And here snowstorms swirl.
Here, enveloped in shivers, are these lines."

ALEKSANDR KUSHNER
APOLLO IN THE SNOW

SEARCHING FOR FAITH

A church choir sings "Silent Night," a German carol that is unfamiliar to most Russians, as more than five thousand Petersburgers pack St. Isaac's Cathedral to celebrate Orthodox Christmas—once again an official holiday across Russia. Surrounded by more than four hundred icons and frescoes, tons of malachite, and shining gold, many in the crowd are familiar with the rites and chants of the Russian Orthodox Church. Others fumble to cross themselves, mystified by rituals forgotten during seven decades of Communism—a time when atheism was the official article of faith. Crackling candles of beeswax and burning incense mix with priestly cadences of Old Church Slavonic. As the choir sings, Petersburgers find comfort in a dimly remembered past.

Once the church of the tsars, St. Issac's—one of the largest domed cathedrals in the world—was used by the Communist Party to debase religion. Lenin's writings were displayed amidst the church's icons, and a 279-foot (93-meter) Foucault pendulum was hung from its soaring dome to demonstrate the movement of the earth and the power of science. Now Lenin's propaganda and the pendulum are gone.

S praznikom! "Happy holidays!" The Russian Christmas greeting rolls off the lips of Petersburgers as they enter the giant rotunda. Their eyes are immediately drawn to the ceiling of the main dome where a massive painting covers more than 8,600 square feet (800 square meters). Painted in soft and radiant tones that seem to glow on even the grayest Petersburg days, the Virgin Mary is surrounded by saints and angels. Considered by art critics and historians to be one of the marvels of European painting, this masterpiece is the work of two nineteenth-century Russian artists, Karl Briullov and Peter Basin.

**PRIESTLY
CHANTS SUMMON**
*Petersburgers to scores
of Orthodox churches that
have been reopened since the
fall of Communism.*

CHAPTER FOUR

The tsars spared no expense in the construction of St. Isaac's, the third church to be built on this location. Shortly after founding St. Petersburg, Peter built the first church and dedicated it to a fourth-century saint by the name of Isaac of Dalmatia. A second, larger church was completed in 1802, only to be deemed insufficiently imposing by Tsar Aleksandr I, who wanted the straight lines and majestic stonework of neoclassicism, a style that projects both elegance and strength.

Aleksandr studied twenty-four different plans before work on the present-day St. Isaac's started in 1818. Designed by a French draftsman, Auguste Ricard de Montferrand, St. Isaac's Cathedral took forty years to build. An army of serfs sunk twenty-four thousand tree trunks into the marshy bank of the Neva to sup-

DEPICTING THE VIRGIN MARY, *angels, and saints, the giant painting inside the dome of St. Issac's Cathedral (left) has a surface area of more than eighty-six hundred square feet. Built in the baroque style, St. Nicholas Cathedral (below) is the patron church for the St. Petersburg navy.*

port the colossal weight of the cathedral—more than 300,000 tons. Its dome, gilded with approximately 220 pounds (100 kilograms) of pure gold, is visible more than 25 miles (40 kilometers) away. Today a few unpatched shell holes scar the south facade of the cathedral's 16-foot-thick (5-meter-thick) walls—grim reminders of the sustained Nazi bombardment a half-century ago. Officially, St. Isaac's remains a museum, holding worship services on only the most celebrated holy days like Christmas and Easter.

But there is no lack of churches for the faithful. Church bells toll across St. Petersburg, for Russia's belief in the Almighty has been reborn. Since the fall of Communism, more than five thousand of the country's houses of worship have reopened. Petersburgers say they yearn for spiritual content in their lives after the collapse of Communist ideology. Frustrated by politics and mystified and enraged by market economics, ever increasing numbers of people are turning to religion for answers. And in the wake of Russia's economic near-collapse, a handful of Russian Orthodox priests have reached out to Petersburgers beyond the golden domes of the cathedrals.

One of them, Father Vladimir Sorokin, former dean of the St. Petersburg Theological Seminary, believes that the church's responsibility goes beyond the country's spiritual needs and includes ministering to the poor, the sick, even the imprisoned. Sorokin gave up an academic post to take a newly created job as director of social services for the St. Petersburg Archdiocese. Now his work is virtually nonstop. During an exhausting eighteen-hour day, Sorokin will give Holy Communion at a geriatric hospital, deliver humanitarian food aid to parishioners in a run-down apartment

house, and hear confessions at a local prison. Sorokin also has organized a small army of volunteer social workers to help shut-ins with chores such as washing, shopping, and cooking. "I don't win any awards for this work," says Sorokin. "But caring for the old and ensuring the future of our young people is the path we have to walk. It is the future of the church."

The Aleksandr Nevsky Monastery, where Sorokin keeps his office, is a traditional place of refuge for St. Petersburg's down and out. Here, priests and seminarians give sanctuary to the homeless and handouts to the poor. Clerics turn a blind eye to those who sleep in a warm corner of the monastery. Each morning dozens of beggars line the snow-covered path to Trinity Cathedral on the monastery's wooded grounds. They are part of a ragtag army of the poor and dispossessed who have appeared not only in St. Petersburg but across the entire country in the economic nightmare of post-Communist Russia.

An old man, cap in hand, pleads with passersby for money. The man claims to be a Polish count who needs to buy a train ticket to Warsaw. His dirty beard and torn clothing speak of tough times and cold nights sleeping in church doorways or a nearby rail station. It is hard to imagine him a Polish count. More likely, according to social workers and city officials, he is one of the estimated thirty thousand homeless persons in St. Petersburg today. Several teen-agers react angrily to a journalist taking the man's picture. "Grand-father," one says, "put your cap back on your head. Don't shame our country!" Another shouts: "You're shaming us in front of foreigners." Nearby, an eighty-eight-year-old

OFFICIALLY A MUSEUM,
St. Isaac's Cathedral (above and facing page) fills with thousands
of worshipers on Orthodox Christmas and other high holy days.
As a symbol of their faith, the tsars filled St. Isaac's with icons,
gold, marble, malachite, and frescoes.

T H E
LITURGY
*of Sunday Mass
resounds through
the Cathedral of
the Transfiguration,
or the Spaso-
Preobrazhensky
Sobor, one of the
few churches to
stay open during
Soviet rule.
Completed in 1754,
the cathedral
served the tsars'
Preobrazhensky
Regiment, whose
barracks were
nearby.*

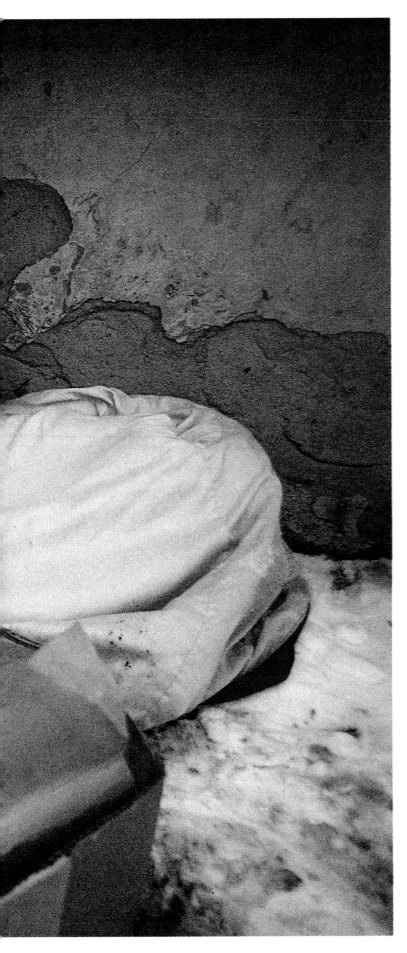

woman in a tattered plastic coat sits in the snow with her hand outstretched. "I have nowhere to live, no relatives. I'm all alone," she says. There is no reason to doubt her—or the depth of public opinion that rails against the dispossessed.

"People still see homelessness as a crime," says Valery Sokolov, president of the Homeless Shelter Foundation, a St. Petersburg charity that provides clothing and food and is building a shelter. "With more than 70 percent of the country living in poverty," says Sokolov, "the Russian government or the city administration is in no hurry to give the homeless humanitarian aid, even aid from abroad that doesn't cost them anything."

In fact, until 1991, homelessness was a crime in the Soviet Union. Even though the law was abolished and the government now concedes that homelessness exists, there are few funds or trained professionals to deal with the problem. Many people are homeless because they have no documents allowing them to live and work in St. Petersburg. Others have no place to live because they have sold their apartments to buy food, medicine, or alcohol. The elderly are especially hard hit, assuming they can get into a state-run institution after they sell their flats. Usually they cannot. The ranks of the homeless also include former prison inmates, furloughed soldiers from the defunct Soviet army, and children, abandoned by broken families or alcoholic parents. With nowhere to go, St. Petersburg's homeless are forced to live in the city's railway or

PETERSBURGERS *show scant charity to the homeless (left), who live in the shadow of majestic buildings on Nevsky Prospekt. Identification cards (above) issued by a private charity record nearly eleven thousand homeless in St. Petersburg.*

FAR FROM ST. PETERSBURG'S PALACES,

a German humanitarian group feeds free hot lunches (above and facing
page) to the elderly, the sick, and families with many children, whose pen-
sions or government allowances have been ravaged by inflation.
Impoverished Petersburgers (below, c. 1900) line up for a free lunch.

metro stations, vacant apartments undergoing extensive repairs, or derelict buildings. A lucky few live at
the Aleksandr Nevsky Monastery.

The hungry begin lining up for a free meal at a
German-run outdoor soup kitchen long before the Arctic
sun rises in the southern sky. For some, this will be the
only meal of the day. The six hundred St. Petersburgers shivering in the subzero cold along suburban
Suslov Street are mostly elderly pensioners, the lame
and disabled, and mothers with sick children. Many
say they are survivors of the nine-hundred-day siege.

It was easier then," recalls eighty-four-year-old
Anna Morozova, a trench-digger during World War II.
"We were young and strong. During the blockade, you
were absolutely guaranteed three hundred grams of
bread each day—about a thick slice. But now, who
can say?" Morozova lives on a pension that becomes

more worthless by the week in a country that is in economic freefall without a social security safety net.
Rarely is her pension worth the price of a kilogram—
a little more than two pounds—of sausage, a street-
corner barometer of Russia's cost-of-living. Like most
pensioners, Morozova lives mainly on bread and potatoes; meat, fruit, and coffee are unaffordable luxuries.

"I am so very ashamed that I have to come here
everyday," says Galina Voronova, fifty-six, who must
provide for two children and a husband who is unem-
ployed with a physical disability. "But we can't live
without this food."

Dr. Larisa Prutovaya doles out soup to the hungry,
pausing occasionally to ask people not to shove or
curse. Trained as an epidemiologist, Prutovaya says
she regularly sees cases of malnutrition among the St.
Petersburgers shuffling through the food line. "I was

trained to study diseases," she says, "but I never thought I would see hunger like this in my own country." Outside the kitchen's tent, a man finishes his soup in two gulps. Wiping the last traces of it from his gray stubble, he says: "It doesn't smell Russian, but it's very tasty."

In addition to caring for the homeless, Sorokin has taken the Orthodox Church in other new directions—St. Petersburg's prisons. And he has broken long-standing taboos, organizing regular visits by priests to a children's hospital where nearly three hundred patients suffer from AIDS contracted in blood transfusions, and to a hospice for cancer victims.

One of Sorokin's supporters is Father Aleksandr Stepanov, a former engineer who used to design fuel-monitoring instruments for the Soviet space program. Now an ordained priest, he has his own parish—in St. Petersburg's Metalostroy Prison, the region's largest "corrective labor colony." A heavy snow is falling as Stepanov arrives at Metalostroy to celebrate the baptism of Jesus by John the Baptist—a high holy day in Orthodox Russia. A sign on the brick wall identifies the barbed-wire enclosed facility as Ministry of the Interior prison number "US 20/5." Inside, more than two thousand inmates build furniture in prison workshops. They have also built St. Benjamin's Church, a fully consecrated house of worship that serves a growing congregation of more than thirty inmates.

With a small choir of housewives in tow, Stepanov passes through a series of guarded checkpoints and

TESTING THE LIMITS OF RELIGIOUS FREEDOM

*(facing page), Western evangelists draw thousands of spiritually
hungry Petersburgers to emotional revivals. Father Vladimir Sorokin
(below), an outspoken critic of Western proselytizers, gives Holy
Communion to a patient in a geriatric hospital.*

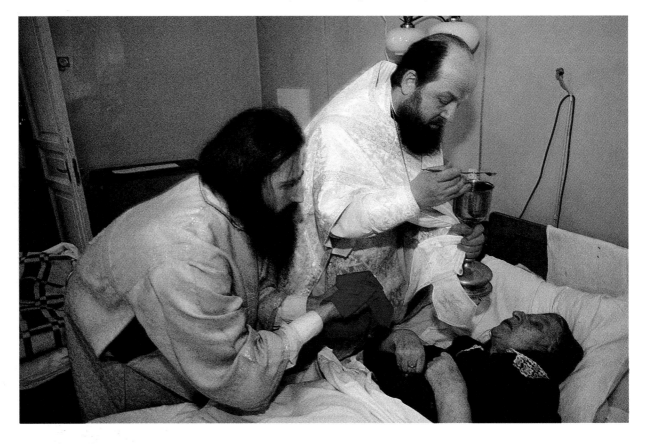

steel doors that slam shut with jarring finality. Several prisoners greet Stepanov with embraces and kisses, including Valentin, the church custodian. Tall and bearded, Valentin has served six years of a thirteen-year sentence for manslaughter after being convicted of killing a co-worker in a fit of rage. "When I first came here," recalls Valentin, who declined to give his last name to protect his family, "all I could do was think of escaping. But now the church has calmed my soul."

Dressed in the prison uniform of rough work clothes and quilted jackets, prisoners recite the Orthodox liturgy while Stepanov hears confessions—a process that takes well over an hour. When Stepanov finishes Mass, he will return to St. Petersburg and visit the families of prisoners, distributing food, cooking oil, clothing, and shoes sent by humanitarian groups from abroad. "Everyone has spiritual needs in these difficult economic times," he says. "In any period of transition, people are more attracted to God

because they have lost the stability under their legs. They are helpless."

St. Petersburg's spiritual revival is not limited to the Russian Orthodox church. "Petersburg was always an ecumenical city," says Father Sorokin. "European Christianity flourished here. Before the revolution, Petersburg had Orthodox, Lutheran, Baptist, Armenian, Catholic, and Anglican churches."

Although tolerant of these beliefs that have long been a part of Russia's history, Sorokin is an outspoken critic of the Western evangelists who have flocked to St. Petersburg since authorities loosened controls on religious freedom in 1989 and 1990.

"For us, this is not a challenge, this is war. This is aggression inside our own house," thunders Sorokin. "They preach Christ without icons, they pray without the cross or the Holy Sacraments." Orthodox priests have picketed evangelical crusades, including a convention of Jehovah's Witnesses that drew forty-five thousand people from across Russia. "Missionaries are coming here . . . and as if Christianity had not already existed here for a thousand years," says Pavel Simakov, an Orthodox deacon who regularly protests evangelical revivals. But Sorokin and other clergymen concede that part of the evangelists' appeal is plain talk about the grim everyday problems of life in a country undergoing a wrenching social transformation.

One of the city's first Western crusades drew twenty-seven thousand Petersburgers to hear the high-energy, feel-good gospel of evangelists Billy Joe and Sharon Daugherty from the Victory Christian Center in Tulsa, Oklahoma. The Daughertys and other American proselytizers continue to draw huge crowds, giving away free hardcover copies of the New Testament in Russian along with plenty of high-volume evangelical religion. "If you don't have enough to eat, if you are having trouble making ends meet—no matter how desperate your situation—Jesus will heal you," Daugherty shouts to a sea of gyrating Russians, their arms outstretched, "Hallelujah" on their lips.

A band of well-scrubbed young Americans plays soft-rock while cameras from a U.S. religious TV network capture the event on tape. Collection plates the size of fried chicken buckets pass through the hall, overflowing with rubles. Daugherty asks drug users and adulterers, the sick and the lame to step forward, publicly identify themselves, and pray with him for redemption or healing. Hundreds rush the stage—Daugherty's "pulpit"—in an outpouring of emotion that is seldom seen in Russia outside the close confines of the family.

"We join hands and sing," says an elderly Russian woman, who identifies herself only as a baptized believer. "It helps when we have to stand in line for food all winter."

Jews gathering at the Grand Choral Synagogue, a Moorish-style building resembling synagogues in

ONLY THE MOST PIOUS
gather (right) for daily prayers at the Grand Choral Synagogue, the center of Jewish faith in St. Petersburg. The massive holy place (above) is filled to capacity for important Jewish holidays such as Yom Kippur and Sukkoth, the traditional harvest festival.

Budapest and Florence, are confronted by a different problem—prejudice.

The once robust though restricted Jewish community continues to dwindle, as Petersburgers who can show Jewish ancestry emigrate to Israel and the United States. There are still an estimated 150,000 Jews in St. Petersburg, according to synagogue officials, down from 250,000 as recently as 1988. Only the most devout regularly attend worship services—about twenty-five men, young and old, gather for daily prayers—yet the synagogue remains the heart of Jewish culture and education in St. Petersburg.

"I love this city," says Lilly Udler, secretary of the Jewish Religious Community at the synagogue, "but I am afraid to stay here. And I dream of my whole family living in one country." Udler has a daughter and grandchildren living in Israel. "People blame the Jews for everything, especially inflation," she continues. "Nowadays it's dangerous to be a Jew in Russia."

Not that it has ever been easy. Peter the Great was said to have had a Jew as a court jester. Under subsequent tsars, Jews were restricted to the "Pale of Jewish Settlements" in western Russia and, in restricted numbers, a few major cities, including St. Petersburg. Those Jews allowed to live in the imperial capital were confined to three neighborhoods. By paying enormous taxes and giving the tsar twenty-five years

of service, some achieved prominence or wealth in banking, medicine, business, even the army. But Jewish students were limited to 3 percent of the population of universities in St. Petersburg and Moscow.

Work on the Grand Choral Synagogue started in 1883, but not before Jews had to amend their plans because of laws that limited the height of competing houses of worship and their proximity to Orthodox churches. When the synagogue opened ten years later, not far from St. Isaac's Cathedral, it was one of the world's largest. But Jews in great numbers did not settle in the city until after the Bolshevik Revolution in 1917. Today, Udler and other synagogue leaders see growing evidence of anti-Semitism. Openly anti-Semitic newspapers are sold on Nevsky Prospekt. A Jewish Cemetery is defaced. And right-wing hate groups with names like "Resurrection" and "Fatherland" hold ugly outdoor rallies of the disaffected, blaming Jews for everything from the birth of

Communism to the country's current economic woes.

It is all the more surprising, therefore, to see thousands of St. Petersburg Jews jam the synagogue for holy days such as Yom Kippur, the Day of Atonement, and Sukkoth, a traditional harvest festival known as the Feast of the Tabernacles. Young professionals, though reluctant to identify themselves, say they come to celebrate Sukkoth because they are curious—and increasingly proud of their Jewish heritage. "Why should we hide in the closet?" asks a university biology student. "This country needs our brains and talent." Indeed, the synagogue has helped foster ethnic identity as never before. To celebrate Sukkoth, young Jews parade through nearby streets carrying the Israeli flag—an act that would have been considered treasonous only a few years ago—and dance around the Torah to traditional Jewish folk songs in the synagogue's wedding hall. The synagogue already has established a full-time secondary school for several

OPENLY DISPLAYING THEIR FAITH,
young Jews dance around the Torah (above) at the Grand Choral
Synagogue. Buddhist monks chant morning prayers (facing page) at the
reopened Kalachakra Temple, which was built in 1915 but closed for more
than fifty years by Soviet authorities.

hundred students. And an American Rabbi, Mendel Pewzner of Brooklyn, New York, has arrived to help energize the community.

"Now that Jews and others can freely worship in Russia," says Pewzner, a member of the Chabad Lubavitch outreach organization, "Jews need to learn their history, their language, to be proud of their traditions." Pewzner patiently recites prayers in Hebrew during readings of the Torah, as worshipers struggle with an unfamiliar tongue. "It will take time," he concedes, "but my goal is to teach and live an Orthodox way of life."

Moslems in St. Petersburg are searching for their own roots. A handful already have made the hajj, the pilgrimage to Mecca required of every Moslem once in a lifetime. The twin minarets not far from the Peter and Paul Fortress summon hundreds to St. Petersburg's mosque for prayers every Friday. And on weekends, about eighty young people—ethnic Tatars, Bashkirs, and others of Central Asian origin—gather at the mosque for what is billed generically as "Sunday school" to study Arabic, the Koran, and the history of Islam.

"This is all part of our revival," says Imam Hatib, a graduate of the Muslim religious college in Tashkent, and spiritual leader of the St. Petersburg mosque for more than a dozen years. "There have always been Moslems here, especially Tatars." During tsarist times, Tatars worked as restaurant waiters, junk dealers, and merchants and were "strikingly visible" among the servants at the Winter Palace, according to an American historian. By 1912 Tatars dominated the city's Muslim community, which supported four mosques, three Koranic schools, and a lively collection of newspapers.

Valentin Tilyashov, a judge turned banker, is typical of Petersburgers who have made the hajj to Saudi Arabia. Generations ago, his family moved to St. Petersburg from what is now Tatarstan in central Russia. Tilyashov's father-in-law collected Korans and books about Islam, but Tilyashov could not read them because most were written in Arabic, a language ruthlessly suppressed by dictator Joseph Stalin. Instead, he studied law. Now in his late forties, Tilyashov has prayed in Mecca and Medina, and shopped in the air-conditioned malls and bazaars of Jeddah for Japanese electronics. His mother-in-law is studying Arabic, and Tilyashov's children are enrolled in the mosque's Sunday school. "You might say we are returning to our

COUPLES CELEBRATE

*their renewed spiritual identity (above) in a group wedding
at the Cathedral of the Transfiguration. For the union to become
official, a civil ceremony is also required, as seen (facing page)
at Wedding Palace Number One.*

roots," he says. "We need this spiritual life to feel whole."

Tilyashov and other Moslems, especially those in the business community, have tirelessly helped raise money to renovate the central mosque over the past dozen years. Opened in 1914, the mosque languished as a warehouse between 1930 and 1956, when Communist overseers allowed it to reopen. The last tsar, Nicholas II, prayed in the unfinished mosque in 1913 on the three-hundredth anniversary of the Romanov dynasty.

Tatars joined Peter the Great's reluctant army that helped build the early city. But it was not until Stalin's rapid industrialization of the 1930s and the post–World War II building boom that Tatars flocked in great number to secular Leningrad to study and work. Hatib estimates that today there are about ninety thousand Moslems in St. Petersburg. About fifty thousand are Tatars; the remainder are of various other Central Asian and Caucasian ethnic groups.

Moslems in St. Petersburg come from so many regions of the former Soviet Union that Hatib has to be a polyglot. The traditional Islamic call to prayer wails in Arabic from the mosque's twin minarets along the Neva. But inside, Hatib delivers prayers and a sermon in Arabic, Turkish, and Russian. Increasingly these days, he also speaks English to visitors from the oil-rich states of the Persian Gulf who have bankrolled the expansion of Islamic studies and pilgrimages to Islam's holy shrines in Saudi Arabia. "Money and taxes—these are our biggest problems," says Hatib. "We live on contributions."

Hatib calls St. Petersburg the "ecumenical center" of Russia. "Holy men from many churches have talked of establishing an ecumenical publishing house because we haven't enough Bibles or Korans," says the imam. "Some of my closest friends are priests."

"To us the cock's crow is just a dream,
Beyond the window the Neva steams,
Night is fathomless—and on and on streams
The Petersburg deviltry...."

ANNA AKHMATOVA
THE YEAR NINETEEN THIRTEEN: A PETERSBURG TALE

CULTURE IN A CHANGING WORLD

The extravagant New Year's Eve ball at the Yusupov Palace is a party worthy of Catherine the Great. Finely coiffed ladies in crimson-and-gold gowns swirl on the hands of handsome men clad in scarlet tunics and elkskin britches like officers of the Imperial Guard. Befitting a scene from the tsar's Winter Palace, couples parade to the polonaise of a military orchestra. The foreign tourists who have paid almost $4,000 apiece for this ultimate view of St. Petersburg take to the dance floor amid tables laid with crystal and gold, Caspian Sea caviar, French wines, and Russian *blini*.

Tonight, in grand Russian fashion, partygoers will see a private ballet performance in the Yusupov Palace's exquisitely restored theater and eat a seven-course dinner, complemented by Russian champagne and vodka usually reserved for export. The only thing missing is St. Petersburg's nobility, which eschews such extravagances these days in favor of public service projects like the historic preservation of palaces. At this and other galas, now popular among a new Russian aristocracy of *biznesmeny*, politicians, and artists, the perfumed air is full of nostalgia for a Russia long gone, for an age of glittering accomplishment when St. Petersburg reigned as a world center of the arts.

As the music of Scriabin fills the ballroom, no one mentions the misery of ordinary Russians. Nor does anyone mention Grigory Rasputin. In 1916, the mystical holy man who held such power over the last tsarina, Empress Aleksandra, was poisoned and shot in a salon on the first floor by disaffected noblemen led by Prince Felix Yusupov. Tonight there is only imitation of a culture lost and, perhaps, reborn. A choir takes the stage, followed by a soprano soloist from the Mariinsky Opera, a chamber orchestra, and, after dinner, a jazz band that plays Glenn Miller hits from the 1940s.

AT A GRAND
New Year's Eve ball in the Yusupov Palace, actors in carefully researched costumes recreate a scene from the Romanov era for an audience of wealthy foreign tourists.

CHAPTER FIVE

This gala is proof of St. Petersburg's long-standing French connection. Beginning with the reign of Catherine II, the city became the northernmost outpost of the French-speaking world. In the middle of the nineteenth century, a French poet reported that the St. Petersburg intelligentsia spoke French easily, idiomatically, as if "they had learned it on Boulevard des Italiens" in Paris. Little-known French authors were the talk of the town and Parisian gossip a currency almost as dear as gold rubles.

For tonight's ball, a Parisian catering firm has imported the best that France has to offer. Young Russian students from a catering institute serve up fresh pâté de foie gras, braised noisette du veau à la Count Orlov, heaping platters of French cheeses, and chocolate layer cakes, with all the style of waiters on Boulevard St. Germain. Meanwhile the evening's impresarios, including a knowledgeable Frenchman, discuss the merits of the pale gold Sancerre wine from the Loire Valley. It is a solid choice to accompany the foie gras, he offers, perfect for the mostly American crowd, which includes a few Russian émigrés who have made it big in Los Angeles or Dallas.

Faithful to St. Petersburg's heritage, this evening's extravagances are reminiscent of the city's highbrow past, when speaking French was only one of many affectations of the Russian nobility. Tsar Peter and, later, Catherine the Great filled its schools and theaters with mentors from abroad, hoping to foster the liberal ideas of the European Enlightenment in conservative rough-hewn Russia. The resulting clash of cultures became one of the great themes in much of the art, literature, and music created in St. Petersburg.

In slightly less than three hundred years, St. Petersburg has been home to writers such as Pushkin, Gogol, and Dostoyevsky; composers Tchaikovsky, Stravinsky, and Shostakovich; poets Akhmatova, Mandelstam, and Brodsky; artists Repin, Serov, and Chagall; and dancers Nureyev, Makarova, and Baryshnikov—each attempting to come to terms with the political and cultural forces that were tearing at the

157
Глава
пятая

CIRCA 1914, daughters of the Russian nobility received dancing lessons at the prestigious Smolny Institute.

city. Many of St. Petersburg's finest minds and greatest talents were murdered or imprisoned when the Bolsheviks rose to power. Others fled or were forced into lonely exile abroad. Under Communist rule, the arts—while lavishly subsidized—were frozen in the nineteenth century by the heavy hand of Soviet censors. Despite these handicaps, the arts continued to flourish, and while the Bolsheviks made Moscow the political capital of the Soviet Union, St. Petersburg remained its cultural center.

Today the city boasts no fewer than fifty theaters and concert halls, including twenty-one devoted to ballet and drama and ten to classical music. They include everything from the world-famous Mariinsky Opera and Ballet (formerly the Kirov) and the St. Petersburg Philharmonic to the Catherine II Erotic Variety Theater. At least ninety museums house collections ranging from historic artillery pieces to the manuscripts of Pushkin and Dostoyevsky.

The largest of St. Petersburg's nearly two hundred public libraries is the National Library of Russia (formerly the Saltykov-Shchedrin Library), where archivists have preserved documents written in Peter the Great's own hand, Voltaire's seven thousand–volume private library, and a special room full of rare manuscripts in Old Church Slavonic. The collection includes the *Ostromir Gospel*, written in 1056 and considered by scholars to be the oldest surviving document from ancient Russia.

In the Old Imperial Senate building on the banks of the Neva, a paper trail of Russia's tsarist past is stored in the Russian State Historical Archives. Closely guarded by Soviet authorities, the collection is only now being opened to Russian and Western historians. Some of the first items unearthed in the archives' six million files were documents and letters that shed light on Russian policies toward Jews during the nineteenth century and others that illuminate the private lives of the Romanov clan. Across the river at the Pushkin House, even more prerevolutionary Russian history is warehoused in conditions that scholars consider a fire

hazard. The manuscripts of Pushkin, Dostoyevsky, and Gogol are stored with the writings of Byron, Dickens, Napoleon, Zola, and Balzac in long-neglected tinder-dry rooms.

But as the city, like the country, teeters on the brink of economic collapse, artists worry less about the loss of culture and more about making enough money to survive. State support of the arts and culture has dropped to its lowest point since Peter the Great summoned the Russian people to build him a capital that would celebrate the art and architecture of Europe.

"Poetry can only be a hobby," confides Aleksandr Kushner, St. Petersburg's best-known living poet, over coffee and pastries at the Literary Café, one of Pushkin's old haunts. "No one can make a living being a poet." This is a painful admission for the poet laureate of a city that claimed some six thousand more-or-less full-time poets only a generation ago, when poets and writers belonged to state-supported unions that rewarded its favored artists with good salaries, summer cottages, and foreign travel. "Our time as poets is so different from the last century," says Kushner.

Author of eleven books of poetry, Kushner makes a living teaching Russian literature, giving occasional poetry readings for international visitors, and from the royalties his writings bring. These include a new book in English, *Apollo in the Snow*, a slender volume of stark verse that materializes from Kushner's briefcase. He is especially proud of a foreword by Joseph Brodsky, a friend and fellow St. Petersburg poet who was hounded, imprisoned, and later exiled to America by the KGB secret police as a "parasite" and "idler." Brodsky went on to become poet laureate of the United States, but never lost his affection for Kushner's scholarly classic lyric. He calls Kushner's work "poetry in its pure form—the purest available to the Russian language."

While subdued by the economy, poetry still remains something of a national passion in Russia. In St. Petersburg, where poets are traditionally lavished with the accolades other cultures usually reserve for sports

*ALEKSANDR PUSHKIN is immortalized in the
St. Petersburg suburb of Pushkin—named in 1937 to honor the
ever-popular nineteenth-century poet.*

heroes or movie stars, Pushkin is the city's undisputed favorite son. "Pushkin is a national treasure, our greatest poet," exclaims Boris Kalaushin, a St. Petersburg painter and illustrator of children's books, slightly surprised that anyone would ask so naive a question. "Pushkin has no equal in St. Petersburg, maybe not even Peter the Great."

Pushkin was only thirty-seven when he died in a duel in 1837 defending the honor of his wife, Natalia, one of St. Petersburg's reigning beauties. Today the story of the duel is part of Russian national folklore. School children memorize the lyrics of Pushkin's *The Bronze Horseman*, imagining that the imperious statue of Tsar Peter might someday rear to life. And babushkas standing in the subzero cold of a breadline will argue, as only Russian grandmothers do, over their hazy memory of stanzas in *Eugene Onegin*, Pushkin's 5,600-line masterpiece of rhyming verse.

Hundreds of Petersburgers also make annual pilgrimages to the nearby suburban grave site of Anna Akhmatova, whose poetry gave voice to the passions and struggles that consumed Russia through much of the twentieth century. Akhmatova, who died in 1966, began writing love poems about St. Petersburg before the Bolshevik Revolution. Although Stalin's censors threatened to arrest Akhmatova if she wrote more poetry, her friends faithfully memorized each new line. Akhmatova's troubled personal life—broken marriages, a son imprisoned by the KGB secret police—and her passionate attachment to St. Petersburg remain the stuff of modern Russian legends.

But gone is the Stray Dog Café, where Akhmatova, Osip Mandelstam, and other avant-garde poets of Russia's "Silver Age" before World War I, gave frequent readings to an intellectual elite that was the envy of all Europe. Now poetry, like the rest of the arts, is forced to compete with entertainment imported from the West, and everything is underscored by the country's economic hardships. Poetry readings these

FILLED WITH CLASSICAL
sculptures, Peter the Great's Summer Garden gleams under an early autumn snow. By special decree, Tsar Nicholas I restricted use of the park to officers and the "decently dressed."

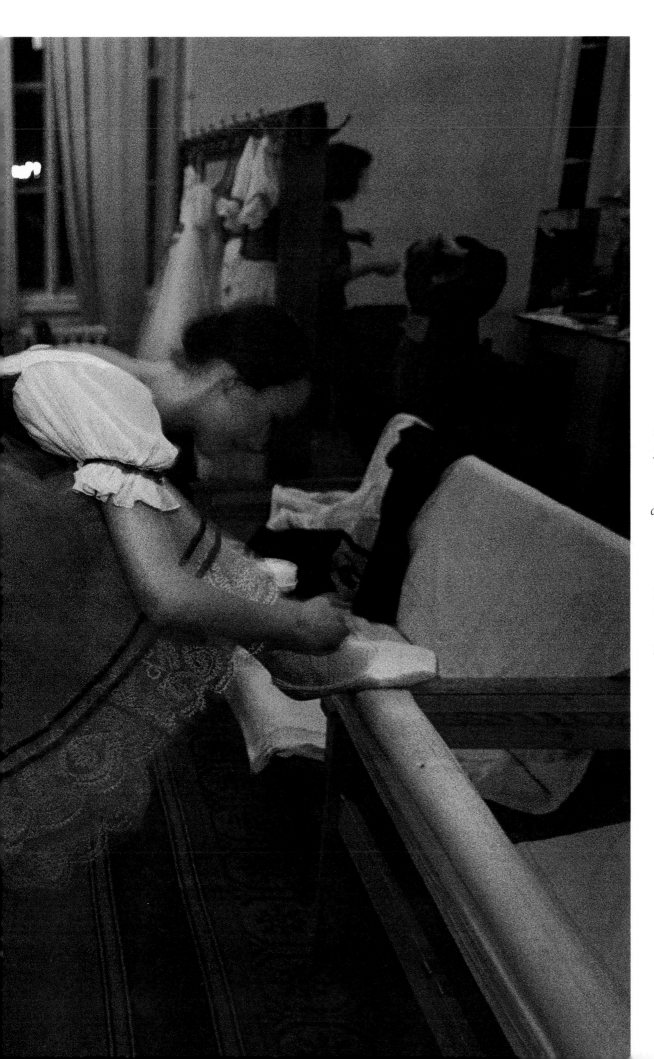

THE
ELITE
*corps de ballet
of the Mariinsky
troupe, formerly
the Kirov, prepare
for the first act of
Giselle. Many in
this world-famous
dance company say
they are weary
of its classical
repertoire, and
yearn, instead, for
more modern pro-
ductions and a
larger share of the
troupe's revenue.*

days are more likely to take place in factory cafeterias, sports clubs, libraries, or on television. Artists who once fought Communist intimidation are now appalled by the triumph of MTV videos, cabaret sex shows, and reruns of American soap operas like "Santa Barbara." They feel unimportant, shunted aside, and almost long for the days of Soviet repression when poets, painters, composers, and dancers struggled against limits of artistic freedom.

"The St. Petersburg school has lost its special place in poetry," concedes Kushner. "The line [from Pushkin to Akhmatova] was broken in many ways—by the threat of arrest, by the war, by the lies, by the poverty of our economy, by the filth in our doorways." Still, Kushner believes that "friendly circles of intellectuals always will exist in Petersburg." But to the general public, the most popular authors are Western storytellers like Frederick Forsyth, Stephen King, and Tom Clancy. Their riveting thrillers are quickly turned into cheap paperbacks that are sold not just in bookstores on Nevsky Prospekt, but in subway passages, street-corner kiosks, and even farmers' markets. Also popular are translations of books about business, economics, and finance and foreign language primers, especially English.

At the House of Writers just off Liteiny Prospekt, the current mass appeal of Western fiction is greeted with highbrow scorn. State subsidies still keep a scholarly bureaucracy employed, although the focus seems

WARMING UP *in the wings of the Mariinsky Theater, Ulyana Lopatkina (right) prepares to take center stage in* Giselle. *The 1,700-seat theater (below) was built in 1860 and named for Maria, the wife of Tsar Aleksandr II.*

to be backward rather than forward. Poetry readings and lectures usually feature the work of artists who are dead rather than alive. Playwright and author Fyodor Abramov, whose plays *The House* and *Brothers and Sisters* have had long-running success with the Maly Drama Theater, the city's leading repertory company, is remembered on the tenth anniversary of his death. But when asked to name the city's leading contemporary—or living—writers, it takes a spokesperson for the literary establishment three days to respond—and then with only vague suggestions of writers with promise. Finally, someone mentions Aleksandr Kushner.

The former Kirov Opera and Ballet Theater, now renamed the Mariinsky, has been called a dream factory left over from the nineteenth century, when the pirouettes and grande jetés of St. Petersburg ballet dancers set the world standard. To publicly advance the cause of Communism, Soviet rulers lavished the Kirov with money and foreign travel. But support came at a price. The Kirov administrators shunned the "ideologically impure" repertoires of Russian émigrés such as George Balanchine and Mikhail Baryshnikov, two of St. Petersburg's most famous sons who fled into exile to develop distinctive ballet theaters of their own in the West.

Now, backstage, the curtain is about to go up on the second act of *Giselle*. And the scene has all the intensity of a playoff game in America's bruising National Football League. The smell of sweat assaults the senses in the cramped "wings" of the gilded theater, where orchestra seats cost about as much as NFL tickets on the fifty-yard line—$70

apiece at New York ticket outlets. Like all champion athletes, the dancers, attended to by a bevy of trainers, grunt and strain to limber up rock-solid muscles. Every performance, they say, is a test of stamina. And coaches—most former Kirov stars—talk soloists through precisely timed routines, their hands and arms slicing the air as they give instructions.

A slim young woman in an Italian sweat suit and pink leggings emerges from a side door. Concentrating intently, eighteen-year-old Ulyana Lopatkina takes center stage, paces off a few steps, and tries a few jumps. She is the star, tonight's soloist who will lead the corps de ballet to a crowd-pleasing finale.

Born in the Crimea, Lopatkina is a skyrocketing talent at a time when many prima ballerinas are fleeing St. Petersburg and Moscow for companies in the West, where the pay and living conditions are better. "I don't know if I'm ready," she confides. A graduate of St. Petersburg's 257-year-old Vaganova Ballet Academy, one of the most famous ballet conservatories in the world, Lopatkina sees the ghosts of alumni like Anna Pavlova and Natalia Makarova as she paces alone moments before the stage lights come up.

Enter Olga Moiseyeva, a Kirov star for twenty-eight years before becoming the no-nonsense coach of

Mariinsky's elite. She grasps Lopatkina's pencil-thin arm and fixes her with a critical gaze. "Don't hide your face from the lights," cautions Moiseyeva, still full of fire at sixty-four. "Keep your chin up! Hold your arms straight!" she orders. "Keep your head lively. This isn't *Swan Lake* where you can do whatever you want!"

A few ballerinas are still tying their shoes or adjusting their tights when a bell rings and the

PRACTICE MAKES FOR PERFECTION
at the Mariinsky Ballet and Opera. Former prima ballerina
Olga Moiseyeva (above) keeps the tradition of the imperial ballet alive,
demonstrating a step in Sleeping Beauty *for her student, soloist Ulyana*
Lopatkina. Newcomer Irma Noiradze (facing page), a native of Tbilisi,
Georgia, awaits her daily session with Moiseyeva.

curtain goes up. Lopatkina rises on her tiptoes, chin up as ordered, and bursts onto the stage. "Go, go . . . go!" shouts Moiseyeva over the orchestra. She and a half-dozen other mentors keep a constant stream of chatter and encouragement aimed at the dancers. Before the show is over, the stage manager is literally counting "one-two-three" to keep the corps de ballet in step.

Giselle ends, and after three curtain calls the dancers leave the stage, the deafening applause, shouts, and whistles of boisterous fans still ringing through the theater. Moiseyeva, all smiles, embraces Lopatkina, kisses her on both cheeks in the fashion of Europeans, and presses a bouquet of roses on her protégée.

Tonight, however, there will be no dressing room interviews. "Too busy," says Moiseyeva, hustling Lopatinka away to meet an 11 P.M. curfew. Tomorrow Lopatkina and the other Mariinsky soloists have six hours of classes and rehearsals before another performance. Moiseyeva, one of the toughest coaches in the big leagues of classical ballet, has the last word: "Ballet is a matter of constant perfection, but my girls become stars."

But being a star isn't everything. Prima ballerinas and soloists say they want greater artistic freedom and more opportunities to travel abroad where they can earn foreign currency.

"Dancers who take jobs abroad don't have to worry about getting the right food or living in fear of riots or coups," says Julia Makhalina, twenty-three, one of the Mariinsky's current prima ballerinas in a company that numbers some 1,500 and keeps one of its two 210-member troupes abroad most of the year. "They can concentrate on their dancing."

Makhalina lives with her parents in St. Petersburg and has an easier time than many Mariinsky dancers, who scrape by, forced to share cramped apartments on minuscule salaries. After a performance, Makhalina says she walks along the Neva and "somehow I am reenergized." But being a prima ballerina is more than a little like being the captain of an athletic team, she says. "I must both inspire the other dancers to be better than I, while with each performance I have to prove they are not. A talented dancer can become a prima ballerina, but to remain in that position is almost impossible."

Although many dancers resent their former colleagues in the West who can earn $2,000 a performance, it is difficult to ignore the steady stream of job offers that roll into the Mariinsky by fax and telex from talent scouts abroad. Discord is heightened by a management that has refused to introduce modern productions by choreographers in the United States and Europe.

Many ballet critics in St. Petersburg agree with the dancers, saying that the productions of the Mariinsky have long been stuck in the nineteenth century, and while modern ballets are occasionally performed, the company's repertoire remains largely stagnant.

Makhalina, who dances the lead in the ballet *Bayadere*, is more circumspect in her assessment of the Mariinsky. "We haven't become culturally stagnant. I would not remove one piece from the repertoire, though we could add a few."

Oleg Vinogradov, the Mariinsky's artistic director for almost two decades, says he is caught between the theater's conservative management and the dancers' yearning for more money and freedom. A target of critics at home and abroad, he admits that many of the troupe's biggest names already have left for better jobs in the West—five of the Mariinsky's best quit on a recent world tour. Still, Vinogradov, fifty-four, says he understands youthful desire for change and experimentation,

IN A
RAMBLING
St. Petersburg studio that resembles a foundry, sculptor Mikhail Annikushin (left) has rendered towering bronzes of Russia's literary greats, including playwright Anton Chekhov. Students at the city's art academy (facing page) learn classical sculpture from Annikushin and others who carry on the traditions of the nineteenth century.

AN ASPIRING PAINTER *adds the finishing touches to*
a portrait during the rigorous entrance examinations of the Repin Institute of
Painting, Sculpture, and Architecture. Formerly the Imperial Academy of
Fine Arts, the institute is one of the largest and most prestigious art schools in
the world and counts many of Russia's greatest painters among its graduates.

and generally he sides with the dancers in their disputes with management. "I sometimes help them get contracts abroad," he confides. "The main thing is that when they leave, they also come back." Hedging his bets a bit, too, Vinogradov divides his time between St. Petersburg and Washington, D.C., where he runs a ballet school.

Vinogradov is considered something of a purist, although on tours of the United States and the Far East, he has disarmed the skeptics by introducing a sprinkling of ballets by the late Anthony Tudor and George Balanchine, the Russian émigré who became the dominant ballet figure in the West after being driven from St. Petersburg by the Bolsheviks. Vinogradov's staging of *Giselle*, however, is in the same style of Marius Petipa, a legendary choreographer from Marseilles who ruled the Mariinsky Theater as "ballet master" from 1862 to 1903.

Petipa, say critics, made the Imperial Ballet into the undisputed world champion of nineteenth-century classicism. He choreographed more than sixty ballets —including forty-six original scores—revived seventeen other ballets, and created whole new scenes for *Giselle*. Petipa's most popular creations, though, were Tchaikovsky's trio of masterpieces: *Sleeping Beauty* in 1890, *The Nutcracker* in 1892, and *Swan Lake* in 1895.

Under Vinogradov's direction, the classics of Petipa, always staged with great precision, remain the staples of the Mariinsky's repertoire. These are the productions that audiences in St. Petersburg and around the world have come to expect from a company whose name is synonymous with a grand Russian style.

Art and music developed in St. Petersburg along many of the same lines as ballet and literature, with artists and composers struggling to find a balance between the "westernizers" and the Russian purists. But those conflicts have little meaning today for students and teachers at the former Imperial Academy

of Fine Arts and the Rimsky-Korsakov Conservatory of music, where the traditions of the nineteenth century are passed on like Holy Writ.

For Professor Mikhail Annikushin, master sculptor of monumental personalities from Russia's glorious past, nearly all of his favorite subjects lived in the nineteenth century. "I'm something of a specialist on Pushkin, you know," says Annikushin, a tiny man with an infectious sense of humor. He slips on work clothes—striped Picasso-style t-shirt, beige safari jacket, and a French beret. An exacting perfectionist, Annikushin was commissioned more than thirty years ago to render a monumental statue of Anton Chekhov, the nineteenth-century Russian playwright. Now more than twenty-five busts or statues of Chekhov clutter every corner of Annikushin's studio. And Annikushin still isn't satisfied. The original statue—started in 1962 —is nearly 50 feet (15 meters) high but is only partially finished beneath plastic sheeting to keep the clay moist. "I'm an optimist," says the seventy-four-year-old Annikushin, who divides his time between the studio and teaching. "Someday I'll finish this big one. But something doesn't feel right today. Chekhov won't mind if I take my time."

Annikushin works in a yellow stucco two-story studio that is a testament to his canny ability to please all patrons, including the Communists, who helped build the studio for Annikushin and awarded him the Order of Lenin. Inside it has all the charm of a foundry with steel wire piled high and a welding torch resting near Annikushin's desk. A few busts of Lenin are tucked away in the corners, remnants of work that earned Annikushin the right to travel abroad when many artists were kept under wraps as politically suspect.

"I introduced myself in Italy as Mikhail Konstantinovich," says the well-traveled Annikushin. "But the Italians thought my name was too hard, so they called me Michelangelo." By any name, Annikuskin is no stranger to students at the old Imperial Academy of Fine

Arts, now renamed the Repin Institute of Painting, Sculpture, and Architecture after Ilya Repin, the Russian painter whose realistic portrayal of the grim life of the Russian working class caused a sensation in the mid–nineteenth century. Annikushin teaches sculpture in the same studios where he studied from 1936 to 1941.

Today, 110 aspiring painters are competing for thirty-eight places in the institute's painting department. The exam ritual, which takes ten days, includes painting a nude in twenty-four hours. Although the model is plump and middle-aged, there are no snickers from the young painters, only earnest attention to detail as they work with color and hue in the pale northerly light that falls upon the solemn babushka.

Once accepted into the six-year-long, state-supported course, says Elizaveta Yelizarova, assistant dean of painting, students may specialize in such time-honored subjects as theater and scenery design, murals and other monumental paintings, or restoration of aging masterpieces. The five places in the restoration sequence are the most coveted, say several aspirants, because they virtually guarantee a job at one of St. Petersburg's major museums or palaces after graduation. Others see themselves going into advertising, a growth industry in the new capitalist Russia.

"Applicants are fewer now," confides Yelizarova, "because young people want to get into business and make money. . . . Truthfully, our students can make a better living selling their paintings on the street." Nevertheless, the old imperial institute bills itself as one of the largest and most prestigious art schools in the world with more than one thousand students. Established in 1757 by Empress Elizabeth I, the institute was called the Academy of the Three Most Noble Arts, indicating painting, sculpture, and architecture. The academy was enshrined in a grand neoclassical building, completed in 1788, on University Embankment along the Neva.

While Peter the Great brought science and military engineering to St. Petersburg, Catherine the Great promoted Western-style art after she gained the throne in 1762, seeking to enrich the cultural life of a Russia that was still largely ignorant of European painting and sculpture. And because she wanted to make art a profession, Catherine decreed that graduates of the Academy of Fine Arts should be spared military service and guaranteed the right to work free of government interference and censorship. So that no one misunderstand her message, Catherine had the motto For the Free Arts chiseled over the academy's entrance.

Over the years, the academy has managed to turn out many of Russia's greatest painters and sculptors, from realists like Repin to monumentalists like Karl Briullov, who painted the ceiling of St. Isaac's Cathedral. The visionary Marc Chagall also graduated from the academy, though most modernists, cubists, and

A STUDENT AT THE RIMSKY-KORSAKOV
Conservatory (facing page) aspires to follow in the footsteps of graduates such as Peter Tchaikovsky and Dmitry Shostakovich. Circa 1910, craftsmen (above) assemble stringed instruments in a St. Petersburg workshop.

futurists were shunned and turned to lesser St. Petersburg art schools for support. The Bolsheviks closed down the Imperial Academy in 1918, but it reopened under Communist patronage in 1933.

Today the circular inner courtyard of the old academy is alive with students fretting about exams and how to stretch their government stipends. Certainly no one is talking about a coming St. Petersburg renaissance in painting. "Every institution has its history," says Yelizarova. "This is still the best academy in Europe to learn the classical methods."

Time seems to have stopped at another of St. Petersburg's venerable institutions, the Rimsky-Korsakov Conservatory, which counts Peter Tchaikovsky among its early graduates. Here at the conservatory, professor of piano Nathan Perelman, eighty-six, has been teaching in the same room for more than sixty years. It's the same room, in fact, in which he started taking piano lessons back in 1923. But today he wants to talk about the great pianists and composers who have performed in the conservatory's concert hall on Theater Square opposite the Mariinsky Theater. By composers, Perelman means giants like Anton Rubinstein, who helped found the conservatory, and Igor

Stravinsky, who moved on to France and then the United States, but began his musical career in St. Petersburg. Perelman says he remembers Sergei Prokofiev as if it were yesterday. And he knew Dmitry Shostakovich, who wrote his defiant *Leningrad* Symphony while serving in an air defense unit in the face of the World War II Nazi siege. "You should have seen it. The courage, the greatness," Perelman mutters. The words trail off into French. "*Une autre fois.*" "Another time."

Today a half-dozen young women, including an exotic Indonesian from Jakarta, are waiting for their weekly piano lesson. A professor of the old school with a fine bow tie and a handsome head of long white hair, Perelman kisses their hands. And like a true St. Petersburg gentleman, he offers a few pleasantries in French. Twenty-year-old Lena Safarova sits with Perelman at one of two grand pianos. She begins to play Chopin.

"No!" shouts Perelman after a few bars. "Listen. Chopin would have played it like this in the nineteenth century." Perelman plays, Lena listens. "Then came the twentieth century," he continues, waltzing across the keyboard, "and, bam! You can't play it that way any more! The twentieth century is more abrupt, more

ORNATE FACADE *and opulent interi-
ors mark the one-hundred-fifty-year-old Beloselsky-
Belozersky Palace, which once served as a headquarters of the local Communist Party and thus survived
the Soviet era intact. Today the palace's concert halls
resonate with chamber music and choral groups.*

forceful." Perelman says of his students: "They're as
good as students ever were. They know the music and
the steps of the ballet. My job is to add polish, to add
a sense of style."

One of those who adds style to any audience of
music lovers is Professor Leonid Gakkel, who teaches
music history at the conservatory by day and by
night is a much-sought-after master of ceremonies at
St. Petersburg concert halls. In a few hours, Gakkel
will introduce an orchestra at the exquisitely preserved Beloselsky-Belozersky Palace, recently the
province of Communist Party bureaucrats, along the
Fontanka Canal. But for now, Gakkel puts away his
notes and relaxes in front of an old grand piano amid
the clutter of yellowing sheet music. "Our conservatory is very traditional and old-fashioned, it's true," he
explains. "But, I'm old-fashioned—a true man of the
nineteenth century. Look! I prefer a German piano
made before 1914." With an impish grin, Gakkel
sweeps his hand across the Steinway's keyboard. "I
can't imagine playing a Japanese or Korean piano."
What about an electric keyboard? "My God! I've
never touched one."

Full of passion for the music of the nineteenth and
early twentieth centuries, Gakkel speaks in eloquent,
professorial English. "St. Petersburg is not a museum.
It is a living town. And our music is alive and moving
with it. We have many meetings with the past here—
on every corner, on every street—and it is a very valuable meeting. We pass on our culture, including our
music, hand-to-hand, from teacher to student in a very
old-fashioned European way. But still, we manage to
do it, sometimes brilliantly." After thirty-one years of
teaching, Gakkel says it troubles him little that he can
not remember a single student who has gone on to
greatness. For him, it is enough that Russian music
survived at all, through the terror of the Stalin purges,
the brutality of World War II, the ups and downs of

East-West relations when music was supposed to show the superiority of the "new Soviet man."

"Stalin hated St. Petersburg as much as any one dictator could hate a city," says Gakkel. "But he couldn't kill the city. He couldn't kill its art and its music. Stalin destroyed old Moscow, but St. Petersburg —Leningrad—was another story. There was strength and resistance here." Musicians and composers survived, Gakkel believes, because they had their own language, the language of the nineteenth- and early twentieth-century Russian classics that baffled Communist Party censors. Gakkel calls it the musicians' natural "ideological innocence."

"Perhaps our conservatory plays an insignificant role in the life of the city today," adds Gakkel. "What is important is not how much money someone can make abroad, but how we pass on our traditions, our Russian culture."

To a whole generation of young Petersburgers, culture is something that comes primarily from the United States. Eighteen-year-old Philip Izvarin, like many of his peers who have come of age since the end of the Cold War, has never attended a lecture on music his-

tory and rarely ventures inside a church. Instead Philip has formed a 1950s-style rock band called the Starlings. His father, a highly regarded designer of new cities and towns, is unhappy that his son is not attending one of St. Petersburg's many technical institutes.

"I tell Philip that he should go to school, get his degree, get on with his career," says Zhenya, the elder Izvarin. "Like most young people, Philip thinks music is all there is to life," Zhenya says, echoing the complaint of parents in most Western and a few Russian metropolises. "At least Philip is not fond of punk or *metalistkaya* [heavy metal] music," Zhenya admits.

Philip, who sports long sideburns and wavy, swept-back hair, is St. Petersburg's reigning Elvis Presley look-alike, a crooner who can make the girls scream when he sings "Sweet Sixteen" and "Blue Suede Shoes." He sings in English, which most young Petersburgers conclude is one of the tickets to success in post-Communist Russia.

"The music of the fifties was forbidden fruit," says Philip, trying to explain the current popularity of Elvis, Fats Domino, and Chubby Checker. "We know the Beatles—even Gorbachev said he likes the Beatles —and all the other rock of the seventies and eighties." He admits that the girls also like the clean-cut 1950s

American look. "Elvis is pure," says Philip.

In his spare time, Philip is brushing up on cassette tapes of old Frank Sinatra songs, which he predicts will be the next American sensation to catch on with St. Petersburg young people now that fast-food *gamburgers*, "hamburgers," and home-delivered pizzas are humdrum for those with money. Heavy metal and punk music, say young rockers gathered to watch Philip's concert, have a bad name. Beatings and drug use are common at hard-rock concerts, they confirm. Local *raketerniki*, "racketeers," also sell "protection" to club owners against unspecified acts of violence, according to local police.

Only a decade ago, Petersburgers who wanted to hear Western-style popular music were forced to seek the seclusion of underground cafés and cabarets that were hidden from the KGB. American music—rock, pop, and jazz—was heavily censored by Stalin and his successors, Nikita Khrushchev and Leonid Brezhnev, who built an "Iron Curtain" around Eastern Europe and the Soviet Union. Stalin even tried to confiscate all the saxophones in Russia to purge the country of American jazz—and thus American influence. Saxophonists were issued musicians' union cards identifying them as bassoonists, but the ploy didn't work. David Goloshchekin, now the owner of the St. Petersburg Jazz Philharmonic Hall, was blackballed as a musician by the KGB, after he joined Duke Ellington in a Leningrad jam session, and forced to go underground with his sax. Today he is one of Russia's foremost jazzmen, playing the sax, trumpet, flugelhorn, pocket trumpet, piano, electric organ, drums, and violin with equal dexterity at what's known locally as the "Jazz Club."

Goloshchekin's nightspot is deliberately low-key, cozy, and understated in an age when gaudy is the only way to describe most St. Petersburg discotheques, restaurants, and nightclubs. On most nights, the crowd is young and well dressed. Women come in micro-miniskirts and American cowboy boots; the men mostly in neckties and jeans.

"The audience gets younger and younger," says Goloshchekin, who over the years has jammed with American greats such as the Dizzie Gillespie, Dave Brubeck, and Max Roach. "That's why I give a little lecture before each set." Goloshchekin tells his youth-ful audience that the "essence of jazz is improvisation," something of a revelation to uninitiated Russians who have known little but constant supervision and Communist Party–enforced discipline until recently. He then introduces a bebop number with a memoir about jazz saxophonist Charlie Parker and brings down the house with the Ellington classic "Take the A Train." But what really brings people to their feet is an original score called the "Sunny Side of Nevsky," a title that stirs homegrown pride in the name of the city's main street and the almost certain knowledge that Goloshchekin has played this before Western audiences.

"We have played on many famous streets of many famous capitals of the world," says the well-traveled Goloshchekin, "but it's always nice to come home to Nevsky Prospekt."

EVERY STYLE OF MUSIC
is available in St. Petersburg. Jazzman David Goloshchekin jams at his popular nightspot (above), while a rock concert is taped before a live audience of thousands of cheering fans (facing page).

WESTERN
ROCK
MUSIC,
*which was heavily
censored by
the Communists,
draws thousands
of gyrating young
Petersburgers to
televised pop-rock
concerts, held at
"palaces of cul-
ture" that were
originally built to
glorify Soviet art
and music.*

"This has always been the city of my dreams.
I want to believe that the dreams are not broken."

ZHENYA IZVARIN

EPILOGUE

Architect Zhenya Izvarin and his wife, Viktoria, are staying home tonight. It has been a hard day for this family of educated high-achievers who represent an emerging Russian middle class.

"Vika"—mother of three—is clearing away the dinner dishes. "I have too many people to take care of," she says, exhausted. "I stand in line to buy food and I make dinner. This is my life."

Vika's specialty is a meat-and-potatoes-filled dumpling dish called *pirozhki*. The family often eats two meals a day instead of three. The staggering cost of food has cut into the good life they once knew in the carefree days when the city was called Leningrad.

The Izvarins own a small plot of land—a half-day's bus ride from St. Petersburg—that they use to grow potatoes and other vegetables to help them through the winter. And Vika has a friend with a connection to a slaughterhouse for better prices on meat. This usual Russian backdoor way of doing business frustrates the best intended management reforms preached by Western consultants.

When Vika heads for her daily midmorning shopping excursion, it is snowing hard on Moscow Prospekt and the family sled is called into service. She stops frequently to inspect both the length of the food lines and the quality of goods at shops along her 2-mile (3.2-kilometer) trek. "I used to carry this wallet around," says Vika with a genuine laugh. She holds a tattered conventional-sized billfold. "Now I have to use this." Vika's purse is stuffed full of ruble notes, her change after buying bread. "Soon we'll have to use sacks for our money if inflation gets any worse."

Vika and thousands of other Petersburgers also fear the quality of their drinking water. Public health problems with the city's yellow-brown tap water have plagued St. Petersburg since the 1860s, when citizens died from typhoid and cholera ten times more often than residents of Berlin or London.

VIKTORIA IZVARIN *prepares obed, "dinner," in a kitchen that is typical of most Petersburg apartments where space is a luxury few can afford.*

FAR FROM THE ARCHITECTURAL JEWELS
*of the city's center, the suburbs of St Petersburg (above) sprawl in
endless rows of bleak, concrete-block apartment buildings that were built
during Soviet rule. Petersburgers hoping to find a bigger or better-
located apartment scan the handwritten advertisements that are tacked
to a local posting board (facing page).*

Today Russian and American scientists who have studied the problem—and issued scores of reports—point to two culprits: an ill-conceived $1.6 billion flood control dam under construction in the Gulf of Finland that acts like a giant cork in a bottle, stopping up industrial wastes and raw sewage in the Neva, and an outdated drinking-water system that draws water from the Neva within sight of open sewers and industrial drain pipes. Researchers who have analyzed the city's tap water say it is overflowing with heavy metals and intestinal parasites like *Giardia lamblia,* which causes a severe diarrhea known locally as "Peter's Revenge."

Critics of the partially completed dam say it will have to be dismantled or radically redesigned to save the city it was meant to protect. "Either we destroy the dam or the dam destroys us," says Vladimir A. Znamensky, a St. Petersburg hydrologist and co-founder of an environmental lobby group called Delta that champions dismantling the troubled colossus. A half-dozen ways of making the barrier more permeable have been proposed, but neither St. Petersburg nor the Russian government in Moscow can find the money to finance alterations of the dam.

Meanwhile, environmentalists call St. Petersburg's water a "cocktail of pollutants"—water so foul-smelling that it drives home the problems of toxic waste every time most residents turn on their tap. The only alternative to expensive bottled water from Western Europe is to boil and filter what comes from the faucet.

But Petersburgers have even bigger fears. "Nuclear pollution is our nightmare," Vika says. "It's a crime

TAKING A BREAK *from the daily routine, Viktoria*
Izvarin and daughter Tina (above) frolic in a St. Petersburg park.
Enjoying a rare sunny day, babushkas *(facing page) discuss the day's news*
against a backdrop of classical columns in the heart of St. Petersburg.

against the city." Russian and Western scientists regularly issue reports about buried nuclear waste from military or scientific research centers turning up beneath St. Petersburg apartment buildings, parks, and offices. The dread of hundreds, perhaps thousands, of "nuclear hot spots" is compounded by concern about a nearby nuclear giant, the Sosnovy Bor atomic power plant on the Gulf of Finland. An accident in 1992 released enough radiation to cause neighboring Finland to install monitoring and alarm devices at the plant.

Finished with her shopping, Vika makes her way home through what is now a raging blizzard to the comparative warmth of the apartment. She makes a

pot of tea and considers dinner, perhaps a visit to the apartment of old friends later in the evening. Zhenya telephones, saying he is about to leave his office to fight the nightly crowds on the trolley buses. He can only hope he will arrive home for dinner on time.

The Izvarins seem unaware how often during the course of a day they straddle two worlds—one Western, the other Russian—at the edge of a now shattered empire, an empire that Tsar Peter once sought to rule and educate from St. Petersburg. And like many Petersburgers, the Izvarins say they have too many life-and-death worries to think much about the glories of St. Petersburg's past. For them, it is simply enough to have survived another day in this teeming and sometimes troubled city.

"The challenge was to capture
St. Petersburg's beauty during a time
of so much social upheaval.**"**

STEVE RAYMER

ACKNOWLEDGMENTS

Colleagues say this book is an outgrowth of eight years of intensive study and frequent travel to Russia and the republics of the former Soviet Union, usually as a photographer for *National Geographic*. That's only partially true. This photo album, as Russians are fond of calling illustrated books, was a collaborative effort with my wife, Barbara Skinner, whose love of the Russian language, Russian people, and Russian culture has opened my eyes to the largest country on the planet. To Barbara I owe a debt that can only be acknowledged with love, surely never repaid.

Like many Americans, I came of age thinking of Russia as a distant Cold War enemy intent on challenging American interests in Europe and much of the developing world. My travels for *National Geographic* during the 1980s to Afghanistan, Cambodia, Ethiopia, Madagascar, and Cuba only reinforced this view. When former Soviet President Mikhail Gorbachev came to power in 1985, I became *National Geographic's* in-house Soviet Union specialist. And coincidentally, my editors had the good sense to hire Barbara, a skilled linguist, to guide many of us through this turbulent and fast-changing land.

On our own in St. Petersburg, Barbara and I rented a comfortable apartment on Tchaikovsky Street. Together we shopped in local markets, stood in line for black bread at the neighborhood bakery, and learned that our landlord was born into an aristocratic family that had served the tsars. Barbara's persistence and pluck got us into a helicopter over St. Petersburg to take aerial photographs, though my twenty-five rolls of film had to be submitted to a Russian military intelligence censor because the city is festooned with defense industries and bases. When she wasn't interpreting, Barbara faithfully brought food, clothing, and medicine to needy Petersburger pensioners who had befriended her during a semester spent as a Yale University exchange student in Leningrad. If there is

STEVE RAYMER
*(left), stands with his wife,
Barbara Skinner, and
Russian colleague
Mike Derevyanko in front
of a Russian helicopter used
to take aerial photographs
for this book.*

compassion for the average Russian family reflected on these pages, I credit it to Barbara's decency.

There would be no St. Petersburg book without the support of Michael Reagan, executive vice president and publisher of Turner Publishing, Inc., and my agent Charles O. "Chuck" Hyman of Washington, D.C. Both have worked professionally in Russia, a perspective that allowed them to see the redeeming beauty of St. Petersburg where skeptics saw only chaos and upheaval. Together Michael and Chuck guided us through three trips to St. Petersburg in 1992 and 1993, giving hours of hands-on criticism, usually at the projector or light table in front of thousands of color slides.

Others played significant roles in producing this book: Walton Rawls, Michael Walsh, Alan Schwartz, Kathy Buttler, Karen Smith, and Crawford Barnett at Turner Publishing. And no one offered her spare time more willingly and agreeably than my assistant Ellen Kohlberg in Washington. Ellen handled a myriad of chores and kept me supplied with research materials, film, cameras, batteries, food, and even medicine that she occasionally rushed to St. Petersburg by international air courier along with cheerful letters that took the chill out of gray winter days.

Literally hundreds of Petersburgers welcomed us, opening their homes, factories, offices, churches and synagogues, and the city's great public buildings. Chief among them was Vladimir Nevelsky, chief of bureau for *Izvestia*, Russia's most respected daily newspaper. A St. Petersburg native, Vladimir introduced us to the city's politicians, artists, writers, scholars, ranking military officers, bureaucrats, and clerics, always with good humor and the wise counsel of a veteran newsman.

Other Petersburgers who unselfishly gave their time, good offices, and friendship, usually over tea or a meal in their apartments, were: Natasha Smirnova, Amina Tilyashova, Tonya and Masha Ratanova, Boris Kalaushin, Julia Firtich, Eugene and Victoria Izvarin, Doctors Vladimir and Tanya Krasnorogov.

At an official level, I am indebted to the State Hermitage Museum, and especially Dr. Mikhail Piotrovsky and Dr. Vladimir Matveyev for their assistance. Yevgenia Petrova, Svetlana Sozinova, and Irina Shuvalova of the State Russian Museum allowed me to investigate every corner of this treasure house of Russian art. Lena Kalnitskaya, director of the Mikhailovsky Zamok, made history come alive in the castle she calls her own, while Sergei Lubimtsev opened the Stroganov Palace. Boris Ometov, the city's chief architectural monument inspector, helped us understand the problems of restoration. Ecumenicalism seemed to know no bounds. Rabbi Mendel Pewzner found ways for me to photograph the largely closed Jewish community, and Father Vladimir Sorokin took me behind the scenes of the Russian Orthodox Church. Nikolai Nagorsky of the State Museum of Tsarskoye Selo entrusted the treasures of Catherine Palace to my cameras, while Leonid Gakkel of the Rimsky Korsokov Music Conservatory and poet Alexander Kushner helped me understand the city's music and literary history. Rear Admiral Igor Kudryashov, former chief of staff of the Leningrad Naval District, proved that glasnost knew few limits in the post-Cold War world. Helicopter pilots Lev Rozin and Nikolai Mal made certain I had blue skies and smooth air for aerial photographs. Finally, Suzanne Possehl and Daniel Crosby, two young Americans living in St. Petersburg, tirelessly pursued facts in city archives, churches, and government offices long after I returned home to Washington.

From Moscow came invaluable help. Longtime friend Mikhail P. "Mike" Derevyanko, who was National Geographic's government-supplied guide on many trips around the old Soviet Union, traveled to St. Petersburg to help with interpreting when Barbara was called home early. And Moscow-based architectural historian Grigory Kaganov patiently explained the stereotypes, nicknames, and myths that have grown up around St. Petersburg since the time of Peter the Great.

In Washington, Blair Ruble, director of the Kennan Center for Advanced Russian Studies and an authority on St. Petersburg, helped me find photographic vantage points and understand the city's post-WWII growth and historic preservation movement. Professors Murray Feshbach, Harley and Marjorie Balzer, and David Goldfrank of Georgetown University opened their classrooms to my constant questions and requests for help. Professor Jaroslav Pelikan, Sterling Professor of History at Yale University, always found time for a meal when he visited the capital, and I was lucky that he did. Jary's advice to "look for the historical continuities in St. Petersburg" was the best that I received. Thanks also go to Mary Ann Allin of the Fabergé Arts Foundation, Vladimir Belyakov of the Russian Information Agency, Bill Freeman of the U.S. Environmental Protection Agency, Alexander Ivanko of *We/My* newspaper, and several officers of the U.S. Central Intelligence Agency whose analysis of science, technology, and the importance of the military to St. Petersburg proved timely. Finally, the critical eye of veteran magazine journalist Bryan Hodgson sharpened both words and pictures.

At the National Geographic Society, I want to thank President Gilbert M. Grosvenor, Senior Vice President Robert B. Sims, Associate Editor William L. Allen, and Staff Researcher Amy Kezerian for their support in undertaking this project. To my colleagues in the Society's News Service who put up with my extended absences, I owe a special debt.

Three other editors deserve special mention.

More than twenty years ago, Bill Garrett, the *Geographic*'s legendary former editor, and Bob Gilka, its remarkable director of photography, took a chance on an unknown photojournalist from Wisconsin and hired me. In the age before fax and easy international direct dial, they expected independence and prized initiative. With only modest inquiry, Bill and Bob allowed me to roam twenty or more countries on a single magazine assignment—sound training for anyone aspiring to write and photograph about so unpredictable a place as Russia. Their price for this freedom was a commitment to excellence in journalism, not just photography. And while they considered physical and emotional hardships routine job hazards, they reciprocated sacrifice with personal loyalty to their subordinates, me included. Both men understood that ideas empower journalists, and supported my application for a fellowship to Stanford University in 1984-85 to study the Soviet Union. Without the tutelage of Bill Garrett and Bob Gilka, I would have never gone beyond newspaper photojournalism, let alone have traveled to Russia.

The third editor is my late father, Laurence A. "Larry" Raymer, who for many years was the executive editor of *The Beloit Daily News*, a small Wisconsin daily. My dad loved journalism—he ate, breathed, and slept for the next story, the coming deadline. Against his advice, I pursued a degree in journalism at the University of Wisconsin in Madison. With his blessing and encouragement, I learned how to be a reporter, to take my first photographs, and to be bold enough, sometimes against the odds, to pursue my dreams. Thanks, Dad!

Finally, every author flinches at the memory of weekends and evenings spent before the computer screen while family life is seemingly put on hold. Our family is no different. To my daughters, Katelynn and Susanna, who have put up for too many years with their father's frequent absences in remote countries, I can only say thank you for indulging your dad one more time while he did this book.

Steve Raymer
Arlington, Virginia

FRESH SNOW COVERS
the Aleksandr Nevsky Monastery.

BIBLIOGRAPHY

A Day in the Life of the Soviet Union. San Francisco: Collins, 1987.

Akhmatova, Anna. *Complete Poems of Anna Akhmatova*. Translated by Judith Hemschemeyer. Boston: Zephyr Press, 1992.

Alexander, John T. *Catherine the Great: Life and Legend*. New York: Oxford University Press, 1989.

Billington, James H. *The Icon and the Axe: An Interpretive History of Russian Culture*. New York: Vintage Books, 1970.

Custine, Marquis Astolphe Louis Leonard de. *Empire of the Czar: A Journey through Eternal Russia*. New York: Doubleday, 1989.

Dostoyevsky, Fyodor. *Crime And Punishment*. Translated by Constance Garnett. New York: Bantam, 1982.

The Environs of Leningrad. Moscow: Progress Publishers, 1981.

Fanger, Donald. *Dostoevsky and Romantic Realism*. Cambridge: Harvard University Press, 1967.

Filippov, Boris. *Leningrad in Literature: The Complete Prose Tales of Alexandr Sergeyevitch Pushkin*. New York: W.W. Norton, 1966.

Gasiorowska, Xenia. *The Image of Peter the Great in Russian Fiction*. Madison: University of Wisconsin Press, 1979.

Gogol, Nikolai V. *The Overcoat and Other Tales of Good and Evil*. Translated by David Magarshack. New York: W.W. Norton, 1965.

Golubev, G. Nikolai Vavilov: *The Great Sower*. Translated by Vadim Sternik. Moscow: Mir Publishers, 1979.

Hayward, Max. *Writers in Russia: 1917–1978*. New York: Harvest Publishers, 1984.

The Hermitage: A Guide. Leningrad: Aurora Art Publishers, 1981.

Kelly, Laurence. *St. Petersburg: A Travellers' Companion*. New York: Atheneum, 1983.

Klyuchevsky, Vasili. *Peter the Great*. Translated by Liliana Archibald. Boston: Beacon Press, 1984.

Kushner, Aleksandr. *Apollo in the Snow*. Translated by Paul Graves and Carol Ueland. New York: Farrar, Straus and Giroux, 1991.

Leningrad: Art and Architecture. Leningrad: Aurora Art Publishers, 1985.

Leningrad and Its Environs. Moscow: Progress Publishers, 1979.

Leiter, Sharon. *Akhmatova's Petersburg*. Philadelphia: University of Pennsylvania Press, 1983.

Massie, Robert K. *Peter the Great: His Life and World*. New York: Ballantine Books, 1980.

————. *Nicholas And Alexandra*. New York: Atheneum, 1967.

Massie, Suzanne. *Land of the Firebird: The Beauty of Old Russia*. New York: Simon and Schuster, 1980.

————. *The Living Mirror: Five Young Poets from Leningrad*. New York: Doubleday, 1972.

————. *Pavlovsk: The Life of a Russian Palace*. Boston: Little, Brown and Company, 1990.

Nordbye, Marsha. *Leningrad: The Historic and Cultural City of St. Petersburg*. Lincolnwood, Ill.: Passport Books, 1992.

Ometev, Boris, and John Stuart. *St. Petersburg: Portrait of an Imperial City*. New York: Vendome Press, 1990.

Pushkin, Aleksandr. *Pushkin Threefold: Narrative, Lyric, Polemic, and Ribald Verse*. Translation by Walter Arndt. New York: E. P. Dutton, 1972.

Riasanovsky, Nicholas V. *A History of Russia*. 4th ed. New York: Oxford University Press, 1984.

Ruble, Blair A. *Leningrad: Shaping a Soviet City*. Berkeley and Los Angeles: University of California Press, 1990.

Salisbury, Harrison E. *The 900 Days: The Siege of Leningrad*. New York: DaCapo Press, 1985.

Stites, Richard. *Russian Popular Culture: Entertainment and Society since 1900*. Cambridge: Cambridge University Press, 1992.

St. Petersburg: Insight City Guides. Singapore: Apa Publications, 1992.

Thurbon, Colin. *Where Nights Are Longest*. New York: Atlantic Monthly Press, 1983.

Ward, Charles A. *Next Time You Go to Russia: A Guide to Historical Landmarks and Art Museums*. New York: Charles Scribner's Sons, 1980.

Werth, Alexander. *Russia at War: 1941–1945*. New York: Carroll & Graf Publishers, 1984.

INDEX

TRANSLATION CREDITS

P.6, Anna Akhmatova, "Petrograd, 1919," translated by Judith Hemschemeyer. P.20, Alexandr Pushkin, *The Bronze Horseman: A Tale of Petersburg*, translated by Walter Arndt. P.26, Fyodor Dostoyevsky, *The Double*, translated by Constance Garnett. P.102, Mikhail Lermontov, *Borodino*, translated by Eugene M. Kayden. P.134, Aleksandr Kushner, *Apollo in the Snow*, translated by Paul Graves and Carol Ueland. P.154, Anna Akhmatova, *The Year Nineteen Thirteen: A Petersburg Tale*, translated by Judith Hemschemeyer.